Some Assembly Required
SEVEN SECRETS TO
BUILDING LASTING RELATIONSHIPS

by

HARVEY ROBBINS, PH.D. AND PETER YOUNG

Contents

Perhaps Love

"Do you love me?"

We were sitting at a table for two next to the window overlooking the High Street.

Was this a trick question? If I said Yes then what might follow? I wasn't sure. If I said No, she'd probably walk out of the restaurant leaving me to pick up the bill. So what could I say?

"I don't know"? Even that wasn't a good answer.

"What do you mean, you don't know? Either you do or you don't."

I don't hold with this two-valued logic. But then, logic doesn't really come into it.

"If you don't know then that means you don't love me."

"No, it's not that." I'm trying to justify my position. "I really don't know. I've not been 'in love' like this before. It's all new to me. And I'm not certain what it is I feel. Can you understand that?"

The point is, 'Do you love me?' is a trick question. There is no way of answering that leaves you in any kind of powerful position, and, surely, loving someone should build you up, not cast you down. If you say Yes, without having carefully thought through the consequences, which is, in effect, telling a white lie just to please them, then that will be taken down in evidence and used against you at some later date, for the slightest of misdemeanors. But for the moment, she'll be satisfied. It's what she wants to hear, and I have supplied her with the right answer.

But 'I don't know' suggests a level of insecurity. She would say a lack of commitment. So what's really going on here? I don't know.

I looked up from playing with the knife and the fork. "Sorry, I was miles away."

So how would I know if I loved her? If I were to say "Yes, I love you" then she might think that I was only saying that to please her, because she had asked the question in the first place. Perhaps what she really wanted was for me to spontaneously say "I love you" without her having to prompt me. But then I don't know when I should spontaneously make such remarks. Is there any kind of guidance on this? I don't know.

"Do you love me?" she asked, tenderly.

"That's a nice question," I replied. "What do you think?"

Preface

A Crack in Everything
   Ring the bells that still can ring.
   Forget your perfect offering.
   There is a crack in everything.
   That's how the light gets in.
   ~ Leonard Cohen (1993) *Anthem*

THERE IS NO WAY THIS BOOK is about truth in the sense of finding the correct way to do things. It is about noticing how you in the moment of meeting can shine a light on what is happening for each party. Whatever that is, it will be different for each person. The wonder is, given our idiosyncrasies, that we manage to communicate at all. That suggests that we have to ignore a lot of the detail, and find what we have in common. Actually, this is not so difficult; essentially this is what we are doing all the time. To make meaning of our current reality, we are perpetually recognizing "This is like that" – where *this* and *that* are quite different on the surface.

Here we are offering you a number of ways of linking the kinds of situation you will find yourself in with some practical ideas of what's likely to work best for getting what you want and for influencing the other person such that you increase the likelihood of getting it. Let's face it, we act in our own best interests much of the time, and hope that in so doing we also benefit the other person. That may not always be true, especially if they are bugging us. If so, then we want them to stop (and hope they will realize their behavior is not to our liking – but that's wishful thinking). Therefore we need ways to get them to do that other than simply running away or delivering a knockout blow! So, as with doctoring, first do no harm. If that doesn't work, harm them nicely, without being rude, offensive, aggressive and so on. The art is to be sufficiently bland and neutral – be nice. Having a sense of humor helps; one day you'll look back at what you did and laugh.

So what do we want for you? We want to encourage you to pay attention to the relationships you are involved with, and to notice what is going on – or at least the key aspects – and then to remove anything that is getting in the way of making that relationship better. By better, that could mean more productive, more satisfying, more creative or more enjoyable. The more you do this, the happier you will be. But being happy is not the goal. Happiness comes from having done the hard work. That's why putting in the effort to build better relationships will pay off in the end.

We do mention being happy quite a few times because it's intimately bound up with our need to have or be in a relationship. So it's worth exploring how we understand happiness. Is it something you have, or is that just a vague description that applies after the event when you look back at a time you were busily engaged in some activity? We will go a little way down that road, but not too far. This is not a book about happiness, it's a book about creating good relationships among family and friends, at work with colleagues and bosses, and in value-driven groups such as churches, synagogues, and fraternal orders. It's a book about how to improve bad relationships. How to form new relationships quickly with people you've never met before, and with whom you're going to spend time in the following days, weeks, or months.

Je ne regrette rien
Everyone has regrets – apart from Edith Piaf, that is. Most people have computers and are familiar with the Ctrl+Z function in Windows (or Command Z if you're a Mac-user), which undoes what you have just done, don't like, and wish to obliterate – forever. How nice it would be if we could apply that

to life in general! Just think of the firefight you've just had: the screaming, the breaking dishes, the finger-pointing, the name-calling. And now, somewhat battered, you regret throwing those darts at each other, for saying, "You're a ***" and that "*** was too good for you!" Once you have calmed down, you mentally rewind the argument to the ignition point and simply delete. That simple Ctrl+Z, Undo, magically disappears those last few minutes. All is forgiven – and forgotten – and your life maintains its credit rating.

Alas, Life is still on version 1.0 and just doesn't come up to that level of sophistication. One of the great lessons we learn (and repeatedly forget) is that you have to live with the consequences of your actions. *Forgive and forget* is an ideal often hoped for but not realized. Disputes within families and between neighbors can drag on for years; no one will even speak to the offender. For those that do, the element of bitterness remains, and conversation is in grunts or a series of abusive or angry confrontations.

Therefore, before you push your righteous anger button, it's a good idea to run through an outline of some possible consequences. You know from bitter experience that the things you do – even with the best intentions – will probably escalate and make a difficult situation worse. By then, advice is likely to be too late. Remedial help? Well, you might apologize. Say you're sorry. Actually be sorry for hurting the other person, for the mess you both are in, not just for yourself. Anger tends to hang on and on, making reparations nearly impossible. Catharsis is overrated; taking it out on an inanimate object only increases your feelings of anger. It takes real humility to change this one. In Christian religions, asking for forgiveness is sufficient. In Semitic religions, asking is not enough; you must receive forgiveness from the offended party.

Thinking about the future is a unique defining characteristic of human beings. However, we're not actually that good at it when it comes to doing it on the fly. Sure, taking time to plan something way ahead of time can yield useful data – on what to do, what not to do, and the likelihood of all kinds of catastrophes happening. But in real time, thinking on your feet means there's probably not much thinking at the other end, in your head.

The road to hell, as they say, is paved with good intentions. We live in hope that things will work out all right. Our wish comes true a fair amount of the time, but not always. Actually this is probably one reason why we habitually listen to stories – through gossip, the News channel, or by reading books, watching films and videos. We benefit vicariously from the decisions made by others. We absorb their experience, intentions and consequences, so that, in theory, we will not have to make the same mistakes as they did. Good luck with that.

Which bring us round to the theme of this book. We've put together some nuggets of wisdom and a few hints and tips about relationships of all kinds, and how you can get better at them. You'll see how to avoid certain errors of judgment, and how, by following some general guidelines, remembering some dos and don'ts, you won't have to screw up quite so often.

The topic of relationships is huge, and there's no way we can cover every aspect. What we have done is to break it down into manageable chunks which you'll be able to put to practical use. The reverse focus is also important, and is an essential ingredient for thinking about managing any and all relationships. It's how to remove stuff that's getting in the way. This could be the bad habits you've gotten into over the years, such as the things you say without thinking about the effect it will have on the other person. It also addresses your resistance to change as well as developing your own creativity, spontaneity and good humor. (But that doesn't mean making a joke of everything.)

This book offers some practical ways of doing this, together with a smattering of 'don't do this at home' tips, because we often learn best from our inter-personal blunders. And by golly, have we made some humdingers. So learn from our hard-won acquired experience so that you can do your job better in nurturing relationships. Not that you're going for perfect; you know that's unrealistic. Just a little bit better would be worth aiming for. Then there'd be fewer arguments, less china to replace. You want relationships in all areas of your life which are more fun, more rewarding, and, who knows, you might find yourself happier.

As a result, you'll gain insights into how you got it so wrong and how to do better next time. You'll have a clearer idea of how others might be seeing the situation. It's not that you won't be making mistakes – you will. You'll be making more interesting mistakes, or deliberately making mistakes on an experimental but reasonably safe level. You'll be paying greater attention because you'll know what to look for. And you'll be more farsighted in thinking things through. One thing you do have the ability to do is to follow through a story in your mind to see where it takes you. And where it will break down or go wrong. This practice goes by a number of names, none of which matter too much. What is important is that you can run through any number of options just by thinking about them, make adjustments, allow for contingencies and then pick the best to try out in reality. The genius scientist, Nikola Tesla, claimed that he could imagine a complex machine and have it running in his mind for an imagined week or more, and then observe what was not functioning properly, what was wearing out or badly designed. Few of us are up to that standard, but it's something to bear in mind. Just going in that direction will put you ahead of the field. The magic formula is "If … then …" where you supply the *if* and let your mind supply the *then*, or a series of *thens*, based on your own and others' hard-won life experience. And whatever happens, you will be accumulating data for upgrading the story you thought would work to something you hope has a much better chance should the situation arise in the future. Given the way events unfold, something similar will probably come your way. Then you'll be able to remain in a more resourceful state and deal with things more successfully.

This will make you seem more reasonable to others, as you'll also be demonstrating a more relaxed and curious attitude to what would improve the relationship. You may even find your old behaviors laughable: "Oh, look at me, there I go again!"

So here is the challenge. It's not about skip-reading these ideas because it's a struggle to simply manage your busy life. Instead, it's about immersing yourself more fully into your life-story, a mental piece of theatre where you are on your own stage in your mind's eye, running the program or script to see where it leads you. With practice, as you do this, you'll be learning the pattern that enables you to generate improvised solutions to novel problems. After all, that's what you need to do based on your own unique life story. As you do this, you may find a smile coming to your face – a smile of recognition, of enjoyment, of knowing that you'll be OK whatever happens because your repertoire of stories is up-to-date, to the point and available at short notice.

CHAPTER 1
The Greatest Mystery of All

The greatest mystery? Easy. That's other people. For example, take Maria in *The Sound of Music*:

> How do you solve a problem like Maria?
> How do you catch a cloud and pin it down?
> How do you find the word that means Maria?
> A flibbertijibbet! A will-o'-the wisp! A clown!
> ~ RICHARD RODGERS & OSCAR HAMMERSTEIN 2ND

TO WHAT EXTENT IS A person a problem? Or are they 'just different'? This key point about how we perceive others needs to be addressed, because much else hangs on it. Why? Because we spend our lives trying to pin down the world, a world that is always in flux, and always denies our attempts at precise or ultimate definitions. We have to make do with 'good enough'. In practice it means that we need to build a temporary structure based on our understanding, our knowledge about how both the world and other people work. This we treat as factual and use as the basis for taking appropriate action. If you think about it, every action we take is intended to change the world in some way. I like to use the word 'intervene' for this; it's like we're intruding into some situation in order to satisfy our own need for change – and without asking permission, so to speak. This is not a problem; we're doing this constantly, and we think we are doing it sensibly, rationally, for the best possible reasons. We do things for someone's benefit – usually our own. We are also altruistic and want good outcomes for other people.

In order to intervene effectively, we need to fix reality somehow. We assume that our intentions make sense, but we can never be sure; we always have to be prepared for unintended consequences. We also need to understand other people's intentions, so that we know (make a reasonable guess) what they are likely to do, how they will respond to what we do. But given the complexity of other people, we end up grasping at straws or relying on stereotypes, hoping to find some clues that will improve our chances. We base our guesses on superficial characteristics, the simple-to-spot variables and try to make sense of them. Mr X stands upright and has a keen gaze, therefore he's probably in a position of power; Mr Y is kind of slumped, round-shouldered and has shifty eyes, so he must be … We all do it. It's as simple as that, and being simple, it's probably wrong. As Daniel Kahneman says:

> "Our comforting conviction that the world makes sense rests on a secure foundation: our almost unlimited ability to ignore our ignorance."
> ~ KAHNEMAN, 2011:201.

Mutual complementarity or filling in the gaps

For me, each person comes to the table as an incomplete puzzle. Let me explain. We start off thinking the other person is a puzzle and that if we put all the pieces together, we'll have a picture of the whole person. Thing is, as we gather information, the more we know and the more we realize we don't know. The person changes from being a puzzle into a mystery, one that we'll never get to fully grasp. In the same way, we are often mysteries to ourselves: why do we do the things we do? Where did that characteristic come from? Genetics, upbringing, peer pressure? We can guess, but we have to live with never being sure.

Perfectionism

Let's get this out of the way, so that you won't be bothered by it later. You are not perfect. None of us are perfect. You are never going to be perfect. OK. Got it?

If you are worried about being perfect, that means you are mentally stepping aside from what you are doing in order to evaluate yourself. You switch between two frames of mind: getting on with the job and assessing what you are doing – based on criteria which are probably illusory and irrelevant.

You don't believe you're perfect, but you probably rate yourself as above average on a number of counts – like your driving ability, your leadership qualities, your intelligence, fair-mindedness, and so on. This mistaken belief has become known as the Wobegon Effect, named after Garrison Keillor's fictional town, where everyone was above average (which is mathematically impossible). One survey of college professors found that 94% rated themselves better at their jobs than the average professor (quoted in Gilovich 1991:77). Another thing about self-assessment: you think you're better than average at assessing yourself, but you're probably not. So, if you're no good at it, you'll have no idea how good you are.

If you're spending an inordinate amount of time worrying about yourself, assessing and obsessing about whether you meet some vague, imposed, fantasy criteria (for which you'll never be good enough), that would suggest that you're not available to others who want to relate to you. That's a key point about building better relationships: Stop thinking so much about yourself, and pay more attention to the other person or people.

You need to become more selfless rather than narcissistically concerned about your 'self'. Turn your focus out towards the world and the tasks you are meant to be doing. If you're always obsessing over what you imagine other people will think of you, believing that everybody is going to notice you in a negative kind of way, then it's time to realize that you're filling your working memory with fluff. It's tough living with people like this because they are always worrying and not much fun to be with.

Because you are concerned about your imperfections – go on, admit it – you think everyone else is going to notice them too.

Well, maybe some people might, if they could be bothered, but they're too busy concentrating on their own inadequacies to notice yours! The people who do notice are those with a professional interest: hairdressers do a quick scan of your hair; fashion experts notice your designer labels, or lack thereof, and so on. The fact that you spilt your coffee on your cuff, or have an oil stain on your pants, well, that's life, and who cares? You fret, but others don't. This belief that others are paying exquisite attention to you is known as the Spotlight effect. That you're having a bad hair day does not warrant others' attention, so there's no need to lurk in the dark corner hoping no one will notice. They probably won't. Just recall that meeting you had earlier. What color were the other person's eyes? What were they wearing? What were their shoes like? See, you were too wrapped up to notice. People are both unobservant and very forgiving. So chin up, and on with the job.

Understanding other people

So how do we unravel relationships? Will a better understanding of them destroy the sense of mystery? Not if the relationship runs deep. What helps a relationship endure is the unending sense of mystery of who that other person really is. They constantly surprise you because there is always more to be discovered. Seeing them in other contexts, with a variety of other people, will reveal different facets on their personality.

Think about your friends. What makes them your friends? What makes them interesting? Is it definable? Maybe you've given up trying to categorize them, and simply enjoy their enthusiasms, even though they do things you would never do yourself.

Or maybe you're the kind of person who likes to put people into boxes. Over the years your categories and criteria have probably shifted, becoming more refined or simply abandoned. So the next section is especially for people who like lists and relish patterns for acknowledging the glorious range of variation in human beings.

Typologies

Over the centuries, more sophisticated systems of classification have been devised, from Astrological Signs to MBTI types – and they have about the same amount of validity, despite what their advocates tell you. However, choosing to stick labels on ourselves seems to be a common human trait, as does wanting our name up in lights or spray-tagged onto an unused stretch of wall. Oh vanity!

Regardless of the uselessness of much of this typology, we are going to use a simple four-part one in this book. Why? Because it's a useful way of beginning to make sense of what would otherwise be an overwhelming amount of data. It gives you something to focus on, which you may otherwise not notice. Why four and not twelve (or any other number come to that)? Because anything greater than four would be pushing the limits of our working memory.

There was a famous research paper published by George Miller in the 1950s which must be near the top of the charts for quoted psychological research. He reckoned that we could manage 7 ± 2 bits of information – that is, between 5 and 9 – though that often seems a bit of an exaggeration. The truth is, that's OK for remembering phone numbers and the like, but is straining at the limits for more complex matters. A better estimate is about three or four – on a good day. Four's nice, because it gives us a 2×2 matrix for making sense of the distinctions we want to make. After a while, you'll find that you'll be able to sort the world according to the basic principles (rather than just going on someone else's reinvented version of this model. This four-part matrix actually dates back a few thousand years; it's constantly being reinvented by people who haven't delved into its history and its avatars and think it's new. It isn't. It just gets rebranded every so often.

The four types in this book are gross simplifications, but we're better off than having no distinctions at all, or trying to list everything about life and other people. Of course, there's nothing to stop you exploring the world of what's known as 'individual differences' and inventing your own library-type classification system such as Dewey's, but that would most likely become your life's work.

The four-box pattern (Young, 2003:279–280) also gives us a way of beginning to sort details about the world:

- What somebody *is*
    - What: their physical description, their observable qualities, their typology
- What somebody *does*
    - How: process, procedures, how to act, how they do things, their behaviors, their processes
- How much *value*, power or significance someone or something has
    - How much: Their status, dominance, importance; their ability to make judgments, prioritize
- How they respond *creatively*, how they think –
    - What if...: The future, consequences, growth mindset, their openness to change, desire to learn, their curiosity and ability to think outside the box.

Another way of looking at this is to think of it as the different kind of drives we have, our motivations. These are intrinsic motivational factors, not those imposed by other people. As human beings we need and do all of these:

- To know what things are, to understand our context, to name things.
- To know how to get things done, to understand intention and the associated behaviors and processes that people adopt to get what they want.
- To know what's important, why something is worth doing. We naturally compare ourselves with others – to

know where we are in the pecking order – as well as judging and putting a value on everything, and assessing probabilities in order to make decisions.

- To know what might be, what could happen, how it could be different. We explore the ramifications of any situation because we are curious, we wonder 'what if ...', 'what happens next?' We entertain ourselves by imagining what it would be like to be other people, by reading stories or watching movies that provide experiences we may not have had ourselves.

Before we get into the nitty gritty of assembling relationships and making them work, let me explain the complications of personality differences: which ones naturally get along, which ones don't, and why. Then we can explore what to do about it.

There are literally hundreds of personality tests currently in use in the market. Some of the most commonly used are the MBTI, the DiSC, the Enneagram (fill in the rest yourself). You may have felt something fishy going on with all these different tests because they sorta feel like they are measuring the same set of characteristics. Well, basically, they are.

The instrument I'm using to describe the different personalities is called the Social Profile. I use it because it's easy to understand and, therefore, easy to put into practice when we start building positive relationships.

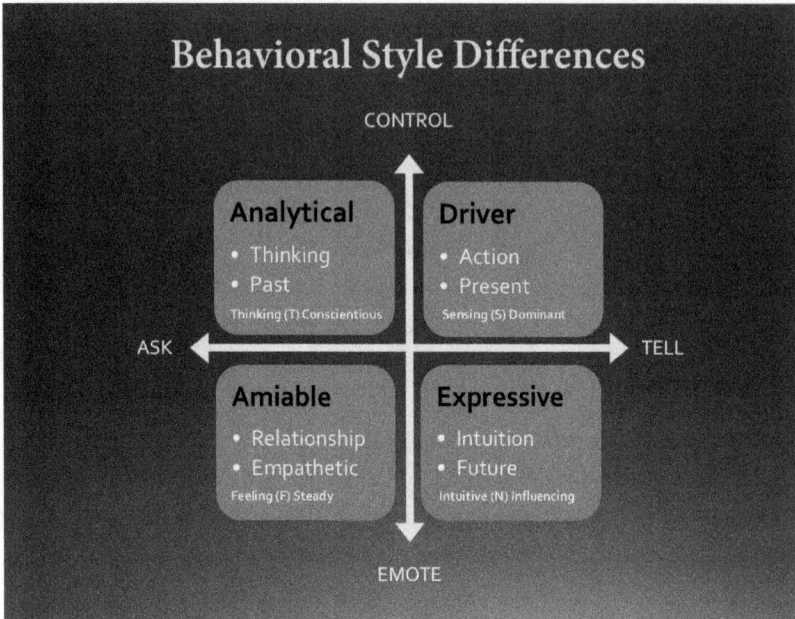

Behavioral Style Differences

CONTROL

Analytical
- Thinking
- Past

Thinking (T) Conscientious

Driver
- Action
- Present

Sensing (S) Dominant

ASK ◄──────► TELL

Amiable
- Relationship
- Empathetic

Feeling (F) Steady

Expressive
- Intuition
- Future

Intuitive (N) influencing

EMOTE

This instrument is based on two dimensions: the Assertiveness scale and the Responsiveness scale. These are key factors when you're thinking about relationships and personality.

The horizontal Assertiveness scale measures the degree to which someone wants to control the thoughts and feelings of another. No one in your life has ever wanted to control you, right? People on the one side of this scale are assertive, aggressive, highly vocal, very opinionated and don't hide their opinions from others. People on the other side of this scale are more laid back, reserved, quiet. They are just as opinionated as those on the other side, but tend to keep their opinions to themselves. Trying to get them to reveal their opinions is like pulling teeth. They sometimes play the passive-aggressive game called 'guess what I'm thinking'.

The vertical scale is called the Responsiveness scale and measures the relative display of feelings and emotions when dealing with others. People at the top tend to be in control of their emotions (kinda like Minnesotans): hard to read, stoic, flat affect. People at the bottom of this scale tend to be much easier to read. They communicate with their body language, hand gestures, facial expressions, tone of voice, eye contact, and so on.

When you cross these two dimensions, you have four distinct personality types. They are really more like behavioral styles since they describe habits or behaviors that relate directly to one's personality. When I worked at the CIA we used to play with the idea of changing someone's behavioral habits (their reward systems) in order to attempt to change someone's personality … Actually, it worked pretty well.

The four 'personality' types are called: *Driver, Expressive, Amiable and Analytical.*

Drivers

A Driver personality combines the characteristics of someone who is both assertive and non-responsive (harder to read). They are action oriented, direct to the point and have a current timeframe. From a negative standpoint they can be abrasive, abusive, dismissive, and overbearing. From a positive standpoint they are great to delegate to, time conscious, outcome-oriented, and reliable. Even though they may leave rows of body bags along the way due to their insensitivity to the needs of others.

Drivers are the task experts. They are results-oriented types whose motto is: "lead, follow or get out of the way."

How to recognize a Driver:
Verbally:
- Gets directly to task, little or no small talk.
- Does more talking than listening.
- Directs and controls pace of conversation.
- Brings people back to task.

- Interrupts, finishes others sentences.
- Speaks in a direct manner: "I want …" or "You need to …"
- Challenges others' thoughts and ideas.
- Asks *what* questions – the results- oriented questions.

Non-verbally:
- Fast-paced gait.
- Forceful, commanding tone of voice.
- Shows confidence.
- Shows impatience (checks watch).
- Cues time to end with organizing papers, putting away materials.
- May seem hard to read (little facial expression).
- Office is functional with a clock visible; displays are likely to include plaques and awards.

Expressives

The Expressive personality combines the characteristics of being assertive yet transparent. Easy to read, fun to be around, creative, multi-tasking, yet also driving for outcomes. They are future-oriented. They want to know why are we doing this project: what's the point, the future purpose? They are great at coming up with multiple theories and solutions, often creating new products along the way. The bad part about Expressives is that it's hard to keep them on task since their minds tend to wander; it's difficult for them to complete tasks on time. Outcomes are just as important to them as to Drivers. This can lead them to believe that multi-tasking is an effective and fun way to do things. However, beware of the macho claims of many people who think multi-tasking is cool. The reality is that this is not an efficient way to do things, as you have to frequently switch mind-set, and that takes mental energy. Result? You soon run into depletion mode, where you can't do anything effectively at all.

Expressives are the communication experts. They are the enthusiastic, influencers whose motto is, "it's not just whether you win or lose … it's how you look when you play the game."

How to recognize an Expressive:
Verbally:
- Talks about their thoughts and feelings.
- Tells stories, shares anecdotes.
- Uses lots of adjectives and vivid descriptive phrases/ metaphors.
- Digresses from point at hand.
- Asks *why* questions – the rationale, motivational questions.
- Persuades and sells.

Non-Verbally:
- Speaks quickly.
- Animated, dramatic gestures and facial expressions.
- Lots of vocal variety – inflection, volume.
- Smiles, nods head.
- Stylish and fashionably current in appearance.
- Moves a lot, high energy.
- Office will be stylish and maybe a bit flamboyant; may be somewhat cluttered and jumbled; they'll have toys and cartoons.

Amiables
Amiables are the people people. Friendships and relationships mean the most to these folks. They want to make sure everyone feels good about what's going on and are included in the information flow and decision-making process. They don't really have a time frame because being so empathetic they tend to be in the timeframe of the person they are dealing with at the moment.

Amiables are the team experts. They are good at recruiting people for causes and maintaining their 'franchise' with others over time. Their motto: "make new friends and keep the old."

How to recognize an Amiable:
Verbally:
- Asks lots of questions to get others engaged.
- They particularly ask the *who* questions – putting the team together and building constituency.
- Listens, paraphrases and reflects feelings.
- May not be quick to disclose what they want.
- Will engage in small talk frequently.

Non-Verbally:
- Steady and even tempo to speech.
- Relaxed body language.
- Active listening: nodding and attentive posture.
- Quieter volume.
- Casual but conforming appearance.
- Their office space is likely to have family pictures, personal mementos and plants.

Analyticals
The Analytical personality is tied to the past. They want to know what you've done in the past that brings them to this point in time. History, details, data. They want to know precisely the steps that need to be taken to get to the outcome and will delay any decisions until they feel comfortable with the process. They are good at keeping a ship stable and preventing haphazard actions. The bad part about Analyticals is that they never seem to have enough information to feel comfortable making a decision. As a result, people get angry and frustrated with them.

Analyticals are the information experts. They deal in facts, data, and details. Their motto: "the facts speak for themselves."

How to recognize an Analytical:
Verbally:
- Little small talk or socializing.
- Little disclosure of feelings or thoughts.
- Focuses discussion on matter at hand.
- Makes very few errors with facts or details.
- Uses a large vocabulary.
- Asks a lot of questions, particularly the *how* – the technical questions.
- Shares lots of data and information.
- May make decisions slowly and systematically.
- May be critical of others who are less thorough.

Non-Verbally:
- Speaks more slowly, deliberately.
- Shares logic methodically.
- Very little animation or facial expression.
- Very little movement or gesturing.
- Formal, conservative appearance.
- Office will be functional with lots of storage space for information.

All these characteristics apply to 'pure' types – which none of us are. However, we all trend in one particular direction: our dominant characteristics. It's highly likely that one of the four will be seriously under-represented. And that may lead you to avoid situations where that approach is needed, or to seek relationships which will 'balance you out'.

CHAPTER 2
What Are Relationships For?

> Gavin: There are two dilemmas ...
> that rattle the human skull. How
> do you hold onto someone who
> won't stay? And how do you get
> rid of someone who won't go?
> ~ DANNY DEVITO (1989) *The War of the Roses*

WE ARE NATURALLY SOCIAL CREATURES; we need each other in order to survive and prosper. This is obviously true in our infancy, as it takes us many years to become sufficiently mature to lead independent lives. Once we achieve inter-dependence, we still depend on family, friends and, indirectly, on all those who keep our society going. They in turn depend upon us to make our contribution. The benefit from this is that together we achieve far more than we could alone.

The term 'relationship' is extremely broad, rather vague and has different meanings depending on the context. We can also think about the *process* of relating: how you relate, how you behave when you are with other people, what helps you get what you want, and how together you achieve more than you could on your own. Some of these experiences bring you pleasure, others not; therefore we need to look at how to avoid the major pitfalls that result in anger, frustration and the severance of connection.

There are two dynamic parts of any relationship:
- How do you manage the relationship? What do you actually *do* – what's your way of relating to the other person or people?
- What's the relationship for? What you *expect* to get out of the relationship – your intention, the end goal, the

benefit? What's in it for you? What's in it for them?

There are two descriptive aspects of relationships as well. The first is simply a list of the variety of relationships we have, ranging from family member, to spouse, to best friend, to team member, to casual acquaintance, and so on.

Chronic vs Acute Relationships

Chronic relationships are those built up over a long period of time. These are the friendships you've had since childhood, and the marriage relationship you enter into later. They are voluntary. Most relationships start off tentative, but once you establish the connection between you, certain ones develop into long-term relationships. Over many years they continue to grow; some last a lifetime.

Acute relationships are short-term in nature, anything from a few hours, to several weeks or months. These are often imposed and are often a result of people being quickly thrown together for a particular purpose. There is no intention to have the people involved generating any long-term commitments to each other. For example, teams and work groups, fraternities and clubs, and even those traveling companions you meet on a tour or cruise. And friendships happen.

Kinds of Relationship based on the amount of contact:

- *Brief* – the desk clerk, the tourist information officer. You make do with a very brief, mainly factual interchange. There's neither time nor any need to prolong this contact because you have got what you wanted and they have a queue of people waiting …
- *Transient* – the tour guide, the person who shows you round during your official visit.
  These people are professionally 'nice', but they've seen it all before, and anyway, there's another lot coming next week.

- *Short term* – you're called in to do a project, or have a technician come to your house.
  During the time you're together, you chat about things – of a safe technical nature, nothing deep or personal. Or maybe, because you're never going to see this person again, they open up to you, tell you things they've probably never told anyone else, let alone their spouse. In which case, your job is to listen, not to give advice.
- *Medium term* – people you need to communicate with over a period of months or years, such as your kids' schoolteachers, the guy who fixes your car, your GP. Despite the reputation that bankers have acquired in spades these last few years, I find that the staff in my local bank branch are exceedingly friendly and helpful. So much so, that I enjoy going in to the bank in person; some things are just not available online.
- *Work-related* – your boss, your team, your buddies – employers and employees.
  There will be varying degrees of friendship here – depending upon your roles, and the amount of contact time you have. Hierarchies often mess up relationships, as you cannot talk freely to those on different rungs of the ladder as a rule. And then your boss has a party, or it's the Christmas Office Fling, and you're meant to be relaxed and open, but that feels incongruent because your official status has been undermined. And anyway, you wonder if this is some kind of trick to find out what you really think of the organization …
- *Long term* – your friends – those from your schooldays, those in the local community, those who share your hobbies, sports, activities … Some friends you don't see very often, but when you do it's like no time has passed.
- *Lifetime* – Family, relations, neighbors. Nuff said.

Good vs Bad Relationships
The second kind of description is based on putting a value

on any relationship. Does this relationship given me pleasure and allow me to be myself? Or is this relationship functional, limiting, oppressive? Does it deny my natural creativity? We label such relationships: Nice – Nasty, Good – Toxic, Productive – Blocked.

We also have relationships where the value is not so clear-cut. Other people may be acting in our best interests, but at the same time they are setting us challenges which they hope will lead to our personal growth and development. They are our teachers. They are being cruel to be kind or otherwise not making it too easy for us, because there are lessons to be learned. Or maybe you, as a mentor or parent, also engage in this behavior because you want someone else to learn from their own efforts. No one ever said life was meant to be easy. When things are too easy, we don't learn the strategies of dealing with the crises, big and small, that beset us from time to time.

Separate Yet Together

You come into this world alone and leave it the same way. No choice. But in between you have a series of choices to make about how you spend the time and with whom. Evolution has dictated the social nature of your existence and no matter how you fight it, you were not designed to survive in isolation.

Psychologically, the harshest form of punishment is isolation. Prolonged isolation is likely to drive you nuts. Punishments like shunning, banishment, solitary confinement cells, withdrawal of personal contact/affection/affiliation are all designed to cause psychological pain, which is worse than physical pain. Under such conditions people become desperate for connection. That's how brain-washing works. During the Korean War, prisoners were isolated, told repeatedly that no one at home cared for them, that they were written off. Over time, and desperate for connection, prisoners would be told that guards were sympathetic to their conditions and want to be friends with them (also known as the Stockholm syndrome – similar to kidnap victims joining with their captors out of a desperate need to belong). As time passed, the prisoners became to believe what their guards told them and, thus, became brain-washed.

In seeking connections to others we must maintain a strong sense of self in order to make those connections more meaningful. Interpersonal relations require a give and take; both parties need to benefit from the interaction. However, if one side gains more than the other, or one exploits the other, the bond breaks down and eventually fails. How many friendships have you lost as a result of imbalance?

Choosing Relationships

How do you pick your friends? With all these other people around you, how do you decide which are to be your friends, rather than just acquaintances? Think about this from the other person's point of view: what is it about you that others are attracted to? Yes, really. What's the secret? Often the strongest bonds of relationships are forged by the fulfillment of mutual needs; you get what you need/want for yourself while providing what the other person wants/needs from you.

Consider what it is that you do for them? Do you know? There's a good chance that you can come up with something vague that sounds good but not too boastful. However, this may be missing out on a key feature – you may not actually be aware of your special qualities which others find interesting. Has anyone ever commented on what you bring to the party? Is it your shining wit, your sensible approach to life, your good sense of humor?

You could ask them. Or perhaps one day they may just tell you. How often do you get genuine feedback and appreciation from others? How often do people tell you about something you do that bugs them? The thing is, you do what you do, you do 'you', and for you that's normal, nothing special. And yet for others, it's something they don't do, never thought of doing, never could do. It's actually quite useful to know what your special qualities are, as seen by others. For example,

> "You tell it straight down the line. I have no difficulty knowing where you stand on this."
>
> "You provide the calm center about which we all revolve."
>
> "You are adept at dealing with people whose feathers are ruffled."
>
> "You always come up with good ideas about what to do."

And so on. Notice these are all 'you' statements, as delivered by other people. It's often the case that our own modesty and lack of self-awareness prevents us from seeing what is obvious to others.

So is having interesting characteristics enough? Perhaps. Perhaps not. What makes other people want to spend time with you, to do things with you? Which people are you willing to make an effort to be with? What is the essence of a really good, close relationship? Now, that really is a secret. If we knew the answer, the world would be a much better place. Let me repeat the key piece of advice: don't think about yourself so much; think more about the other person and appreciate them for being who they are – without wanting to change them.

Creative and Balanced Relationships

For a relationship to work, there needs to be some kind of matching. You might think, given the folk-wisdom of relationships, that there is something to the belief that *opposites attract.* Suddenly you are given a glimpse of a completely different world from the one you're used to. The grass really is greener there; you want to try it out. It's a bit like going on vacation in someone else's version of the world. It's probably a great place to visit but the truth will dawn on you soon enough that you wouldn't want to live there. It's unlikely that such relationships last; the other person will drive you mad with their obsessive cleaning or their open-house policy if that's not your style.

Good relationships happen when the missing pieces of one person are filled by the existing pieces of their partner, and vice versa; both become more complete people. We do not want to live with clones of ourselves. So do we unwittingly choose partners who are able to fill in the gaps in our own abilities? For example, if you are not so good at social skills, then you could team up with someone who likes to demonstrate their superior inter-personal habits? Of course, there is the ever-present danger that you will become their experiment to see if they can teach you, fix you, bring you up to standard. If this is something you want and enjoy, it's win-win. So consider this: you live with someone whom you believe you can raise up to your standards. You want to change them. Not so easy. They have to want to change. Which leads us into paradox country. Remember the old joke, "How many psychologists does it take to change a lightbulb? One, but it really has to want to change."

How open to change are you? Over the long term, you both need to grow at roughly the same rate. If one partner is kinda resistant, while the other is leaping ahead, the gap between you is going to pose a possible threat to the relationship. So it's a good idea if both people match at the level of openness to doing new things, being creative. On our own we often resist change and innovation; what's missing is the spark that gets us going. To have a more interesting life, you need to be with people who provide that spark. As your creative juices start to flow, you'll trigger something in them. Other times, you'll be the sparky one. This is not necessarily something you can plan on consciously controlling – what turns other people on is often a mystery to them as well as you.

CHAPTER 3
Who's Good At Relationships?

BEING A TOURIST
What do you have in your scrap-book album of
memories of relationships?

Sometimes we behave as if we are tourists in our own lives.
We seek ever more sensory experiences, tick them off the
bucket list and then move on to the next item. We collect
memories – the good, the bad and the ugly – just like we collect
snapshots or selfies to show the folks back home. But that's
as far as it goes. These pictures and stories are what they are
– opportunities for contributing to a conversation – especially
those bragging conversations where you're trying to go one
better than everyone else. It's not often that anyone goes beyond
the superficial, like, *How did you respond to those experiences?*
Or *How did that change your life?* Do you want more depth, or
are you happy with the equivalent of someone clicking on your
Like/Dislike button. Conversations often move fast, because
people want to talk rather than listen. They pick up a cue from
what you say – it's triggered one of their memories – and then
as soon as possible they take over the conversation because they
have something much better to say.

So what would it be like if you broke this pattern, practiced
your listening skills, and asked for more information. "Did you
really do that? So what happened then?" "Do you have any
regrets?" and so on. (Of course, you have to do this in a genuine
mode of enquiry, or they'll think you're mocking them.) Most
of what other people say can be interesting if you find out what
makes it interesting for them. In this way, you are taking the
time to explore their reality, revealing their secrets, by going

a bit deeper. This in turn builds stronger foundations for the relationship because you're showing that you care. It may take a while for the other person to catch on to doing it back to you, so you will have to be patient, and wait for their cue that says it's time to reveal more of your own personal history. What if it never comes? Well, you move on. Plenty more people in the world. You'll probably find that you're happier being with those other people you match in conversational style. Some relationships do not venture far beyond the safe and superficial. You know who your best friends are because you'll feel OK to go much deeper with them.

Being curious is for many people a really important quality, and one we don't normally think about. We've been told off as children for being nosy, stickybeaking, poking your nose in where it don't belong, and so on. But being curious is natural; it's the lubrication of a relationship. Just talking endlessly about yourself is boring, not only to the other person, but eventually to you. You've heard it all before; your stories are like the picture postcards you buy from the rack. They don't leave much space on the back for telling the real story. Wish you were here? No, it's much more complicated than that, a much bigger story, the story of who you really are. And your story can be told from a number of different angles; there's no need to repeat yourself. Be curious about your own life: why did you do what you did? What was the real reason?

Good Relationships

We think that being curious and listening is an essential part of creating good relationships. So what else? There are many other things to consider, so take a moment to think about what you mean by a good relationship? Jot down some ideas:

-
-

•

•

Your definition will depend very much on the general ways in which you organize your life, and what you expect other people to do. So a relationship is good when the other person …

• arrives on time, turns up when they say they will
• remembers to return your books, CDs, tools …
• keeps their mouth closed when eating,
• doesn't keep borrowing your stuff without asking …

Consider the people you really want to spend time with. This is because …? Again, make a list of what benefit they bring into your life.

•

•

•

•

For example:

• They make you laugh, they inspire you, entertain you, care for you, care about you, ask about you …
• They allow you to be yourself, to act natural rather than having to adopt a special style for visitors.
• They are the kind of people who whenever you meet them again, after weeks or years, it's as if no time has passed at all.

Whom do you admire, respect, idolize?

You are probably much better at evaluating others. And it probably doesn't take you long to do that. Like, would you believe, ten seconds? Too long? First glance. Yes, some of the time, we can be pretty accurate at summing up another person's ability. This is why we have the saying about First Impressions. So the question is, can you fake it? What do you think? Maybe, maybe not. It's hard covering up the real you, regardless of your attempts to conceal. If you wear a uniform of some description – from designated work togs to a business suit – that will have an effect. And your adopted status will make a difference too (see chapter 7).

Inspiration

What do you see in others that inspires you? People have always wanted to be known, liked and have monuments erected to them. These days there is an increasing desire to be famous just for being famous; brush up your ego, you too can be a star. The rest of us want to see them crash and burn! Is that because we're jealous (or indifferent, if you are of a certain age), or does such a display of talent (or lack of it) make you want to prove that you can do as well or better?

Many people just entertain us. In the moment we are moved, impressed, feel empathy for them. But this passes. We don't want whatever that was for ourselves – we're happy to let it lie with the other person. For a start, it's not our cup of tea – not everyone wants to be a singer or basketball player – nor are we willing to put in the hard work to achieve their level of competence. I'd love to be able to play the guitar with proficiency, but I'm not willing to put in the 10,000 hours of practice to be minimally competent. So, I'm good with watching and appreciating other people's skills on display.

When we see something we wish ourselves to become – we'll go to extraordinary lengths to achieve it. Take a moment to think

back through your life to those people you can still remember
who did inspire you (if you've forgotten, then they can't have
been that significant). Make a list.

- Those people with whom you spent time – just so you
  could be in their company.
- People you never met – in the media or public gaze – but
  would have liked to. Could even be an historical figure
  or a fictional character in a book, movie or TV show.
- Friends, relatives, or ancestors who made an impact on
  the world in some way, which you feel now is part of you
  and needs to be fulfilled.

So what is it about these people that you would wish to model,
emulate, or be like?
(Note: If this doesn't apply to you, then what are you missing or
lacking in your life?)

You're looking for the essence of what they did, an app that
you might install in your own being, a simple reminder to do
something different.

And now imagine yourself actually having those qualities, those
skills, that way of being. How would your life be different?
Would you actually want to change places with that person, and
to some extent, live *their* life? If not, what puts you off?

For most people, there's no place like home. But that doesn't
mean you can't take on some aspect of those other inspirational
people. You probably did this when you were a teenager. So
what's to say you can't go on doing it? Because if you do,
you may find your life changing for the better, your way of
relating to others improving. In appreciating others you are also
honoring yourself. And when that happens, relationships thrive
as each party finds the other more interesting.

Your challenge is to keep every relationship richly inspiring and
continuously growing. It's not something you do to others, it's

about you following your own passions and interests, pursuing your learning, your progress towards mastery of whatever it is that fascinates you. It may not be the thing that interests others, but what they do recognize is the way you engage with your life, the energy and commitment you put into your way of living.

CHAPTER 4
The Quest for Happiness

"... And they lived happily ever after."

THERE IS A WHOLE INDUSTRY nourishing the myth – and it is only a myth – of the Perfect Relationship. One version begins with the Hollywood meet-cute, traverses the trials and tribulations of indecision and misinterpretation, to the climax of the perfect wedding. It's at that point, as a way of reaching some kind of closure, that you get the punchline: "And they lived happily ever after."

If only that were true. If only you could relax your guard and coast through the rest of your life, happy in the knowledge that everything will turn out OK. Or rather, thank God that it's not true. How boring life could become after such a send-off if it was intended to continue running on autopilot. It would be downhill all the way as boredom set in. We human beings need and seek constant stimulation and innovation. Without it we atrophy and die.

A relationship is more a shared journey than a one-off event. The question you are asking, implicitly, is are you willing to literally go along with someone else, to share their journey as they share yours? For how long would that be a reasonable thing to do? You hope forever, but experience tells you that it's highly likely that there will come a time when your paths diverge. If so, what happens then? Time for the pre-nup?

Getting together is just the beginning. You know this. Life is full of new beginnings. Although these are often fraught with difficulties, hesitations, even fear, it's the part that's relatively easy – or rather, less difficult than what follows. There's something about the first flush of attraction – that hormonal rush, the dreams, the fantasies – that sways your judgment and leads you to making a decision about initiating what you hope will be your forever relationship. It's what happens after you've committed that requires more deliberate planning, because then you're just not sure of the best way to proceed. You're setting out on an adventure which you both hope will last long enough to give you satisfying experiences of what life has to offer: parenthood, personal growth, while still finding your partner interesting and wanting to share new things together. That's why we set up various projects and challenges, why we seek new ideas, try new behaviors, explore new ways of relating.

You hope things will develop spontaneously. You expect the other person will naturally behave in a certain way (because you assume they are just like you), but you fail to take into account that everyone has their own way of making sense of the world and of responding to it. It's unrealistic to expect other people to act according to your unwritten and unspoken rules. Why should they? They are not privy to your inner workings of the mind. There is a fear that if you state what you want, then you'll never know if your partner is doing things because they really want to, or just because you have said so. But you dare not ask about this, and so you'll never be sure whether their behavior is genuine.

There's a simple solution to this: make your rules, beliefs, values and so on explicit. This is not just a one-way thing – or it shouldn't be. Both need to take responsibility for growing the relationship, and that means talking openly about needs and expectations, and exploring what is in your best interests. You might think it's embarrassing or scary to open yourself up like this. The fear is that others will take advantage of you. Usually they don't; they're more likely to respect you. In revealing your thoughts you make it safe for them to talk about these things, because they realize that in some ways people are very much alike in how they think. Hopefully you have teamed up with someone who has their wits about them, and matches your level of care and concern for building the relationship. If there's a mismatch, if you're in it on your own because the other person is not pulling their weight, then the relationship is unbalanced and may not last beyond a trial period.

Therefore, if you want rewarding and creative relationships then further action on your part is necessary. In other words, some assembly is required. You get what you ask for … so ask for it. Screwdriver please.

CHAPTER 5
Happiness (or is it Hell) is Other People

MOST OF US THINK THAT being happy is the primary goal in life. We seek others with whom to engage in order to make this happiness a reality. Unfortunately, the other person has got you down as their source of happiness. So you go at each other screaming inside your head, "Make me happy … dammit!"

There is plenty of research to support the concept that building better relationships will, indeed, lead to a sense of happiness. It's also true that you'll live longer healthier lives when engaged in mutually satisfying relationships. Those without these relationships tend to rot on the vine and live 'lives of quiet desperation', die younger, and in declining health. Having positive relationships is good for you.

When you look closely at this you realize that no matter how hard you try, you cannot be happy in every situation and at all times. But then, *trying* to be happy is self-defeating, because every moment you notice you are not yet happy strikes a negative note and down goes your happiness rating. So better to delete 'being happy' from your list of desired goals.

The psychologist Fred Herzberg came up with a very interesting theory of motivation. He reckoned there were two key aspects to motivation, two factors that influenced why people did things. On one side he had *motivating factors* – the things you wanted and would move towards. And on the other were *hygiene factors* – which were, in essence, those things you would expect to have in order to do your job, such as a safe working environment. In Chapter 3 you created a list of expectations about a good relationship. Those kinds of qualities are similar to Herzberg's Hygiene Factors. You expect nothing less. So what would be the equivalent Motivating factors that you could latch onto that someone else demonstrates?

Herzberg's theory was that while we all want to be motivated, not everything gets us there. Sometimes we can live with the situation if it's 'good enough'. At work, for example, as long as we feel that we're getting paid fairly we're not unmotivated. We're satisfied because it's what we expect. However, if we feel that we're not being fairly paid, we become dissatisfied and demotivated. If these hygiene factors are not in place, we complain or we leave. What motivates us are things like being acknowledged for our good work, getting positive feedback, feeling engaged in the outcomes as a valued employee.

In terms of happiness, we can look at a similar sort of model. We all have a certain level of satisfaction we get out of being with those around us. We expect that. We may not be happy, but at least we're not unhappy. However, if our expectations from those around us are not met, we become unhappy. If people treat us beyond our expectations, we move above the line and are really happy. For a while. Soon it becomes the new normal; expectations rise.

Our happiness, however, depends not just on how we're treated by others, whether they meet our expectations or not, but by confounding factors like body chemistry: How much sleep you got (melatonin levels), what/when you last ate (blood sugar levels), good/bad news (serotonin levels), and so on. Biologically, we're all over the place. And don't even mention hormone levels. Our perception of what makes us happy in the moment is controlled by factors both inside and outside our control.

We all rub along together in a world that leads us to think, "Well, at least it's not all that bad. Could be worse." We learn to live with satisfaction (below the line) but truly desire happiness (above the line). One way to ensure that you spend more time above the line is to lower your expectations, both of others and of yourself. It's great to have elevated expectations, and to set your personal and professional goals high, because these provide a great driving force. When you do achieve them, they're something you can be proud of. However, some people are never satisfied even when they reach their lofty goals. Stress rules their lives – they worry about maintaining their high position – and they cannot become happy no matter what they (or others) do.

In practical terms, having reduced expectations means: don't expect your spouse to bring you flowers every day. That way, when they do, you're happy; don't expect your kid to be a genius (although you probably push him or her to be) so when they get great grades, you're happy (just remember to tell them that you're happy with their effort they put in to achieve that outcome). Lowering expectations won't make you happy all the time, but at least you won't be unhappy as often. Give yourself (and others) a break. Being satisfied is not happiness, but at least it's not the end of the world.

Happiness comes after

It is unrealistic to hold the achievement of happiness as a worthy pursuit. Happiness is more a byproduct of your inputs into the relationship. When you think back you notice that you were happy only *after* the event, not while you were deeply engaged in that activity. At the time, you were too busy getting on with it, so focused – in the zone or in a state of flow – that you did not have any spare mental capacity to think, "Oh, I'm happy now!" Taking time to evaluate how you're feeling is an interruption that switches you out of the moment. Constantly checking on your level of happiness means you are going to be constantly flipping from one state of mind to another, and that is not a recipe for happiness.

Now you could look back at your life, those times with other people which you think of as happiness, or bliss, or whatever, and wonder: What was it I was actually doing? What exactly was the cause of my happiness then? Even if you were to set up the self-same conditions, there's no guarantee that you'll feel happy the next time. The fact that you were doing something for the first time could be a factor. Then the second time you have expectations, modified by the first time. Too much thinking about it! Better to stop clocking your activities, and be more fully in the present. Stop thinking about yourself and your state, and pay more attention to the other person or people you are with. Are they happy? Listen to them, just be with them, caring more about them and their needs. Or simply get lost in the shared moment, enjoying the interaction. That way you're more likely to find, later, that it was a happy experience – especially if at the time it was intense or felt challenging.

If you're feeling miserable at the moment – a major relationship is not working out, or you're feeling pressured to do things or be things that don't match your values – give yourself some 'me-time' (see Chapter 35) to think through the ideas in this book. Identify things you have done in the past that have been effective in changing your state. These will probably work for you now, too. Most important is actually deciding to do something, to get yourself out of your slump, overcome your inertia.

Dunk that madeleine, or How to make yourself unhappy

One way of passing the time is to rewrite the history of your life in ways that you think would have produced a more satisfactory outcome. Which is to say, something different from what you actually have right now. Why are we so dissatisfied with our lives? Is it because we have unrealistic expectations? We thought that learning the art of forming and maintaining relationships would be easy, but being learners – and given the way of the world – nothing quite turned out the way we thought it would.

> "There's nothing about the basic concept
> behind Facebook that I couldn't have
> dreamed up myself – and yet I can't help
> noticing it's Mark Zuckerberg, not me,
> with the net worth of $50bn."
> ~ OLIVER BURKEMAN (2015)

Let's take a different route: "If only I'd known then, what I know now" as a starting point. It's wishful thinking. Sure, you could have bought up acres of real estate for a song, or invested in companies during their start-up phase and made a fortune – but you didn't. You didn't recognize the signs, nor did anyone else at the time, because you lacked a crystal ball. The second part of this fantasy is to imagine that if you had done whatever, you would have been happier. Does that sound reasonable? Really? How would you know? You don't know. There are many paths not taken through that grass that's always greener. OK, it's cliché time, but they're based on everyday life experience. Every decision has what is known as an opportunity cost – what you could have done instead. But you made your choices – and who knows, you may have chosen exactly the right path for you at that time. Another way to look at it is to believe that it doesn't really matter which path you take – you'll still have ended up in pretty much the same place. Wherever you go, there you are. So how are you changing? The one constant is you, the person making the journey.

We're good at inventing false futures as well. We run many fantasy movies in our minds. Sometimes this is a form of mental rehearsal – so we'll be better able to respond to life's contingencies. But many are just fantasies, and it's probably a good thing they don't come true, especially those which involve other people. Because of our limited imagination, we would miss out on the surprises, the interesting bits. If we were stuck with events happening exactly the way we imagined them, we'd be disappointed. How tedious would that be: no unexpected benefits, no bonuses. In other words, rather dull.

CHAPTER 6
Toxic Relationships

THERE ARE 7.13 BILLION UNIQUE individuals inhabiting our planet. Although we make life simpler by lumping whole swathes of folk together, when we meet them face-to-face we realize just how many differences there are. What's more, other people pick up on different differences, so that, for example, someone who seems like a creep to you may not come across as creepy to another person. You've probably noticed something like this about other people's relationships: "Whatever does she see in him?" or "Can you imagine living with a woman like that? I can't."

We appreciate variety. After all, you would not want to live with a clone of yourself. Instead, you want others to maintain an air of mystery to some degree. However, you will no doubt have come across other people who are unfathomable. They think in a very different way from you; like they're from another planet. Trouble is, these folk co-exist in your world. Try as you might, finding a way to relate to these aliens taxes your social skills to the limit. There is a commonly used term to describe these relationships: toxic. You are never going to see eye-to-eye with these people. They also end up working in your companies and are members of your teams. You probably have found them easy to spot because they just don't behave normally – which is to say, just like you do. You're never going to be best buddies, so you either have to distance yourself from them – get them off your team, out of your organization, or out of your house – or learn to live with them by understanding a little of what's actually going on here. So, what's the secret of getting along with everyone else? It's a trick known as versatility.

Given the four general styles, you would guess that some get along nicely (compatible relationships) while some would rather eat nails than be in the same room together (toxic relationships). Let me to tell a story that actually happened many years ago to illustrate my point about toxic relationships.

After being married for eight years, my wife Nancy and I decided we'd like to design and build our own house in the woods in Minnetonka, Minnesota. My wife is a Driver and I am an Expressive. Needless to say, the experience was memorable. When the house was completed, I felt that there was something missing, but couldn't quite figure out what. So, being intuitive (as most Expressives are), I thought that if I drove around some nearby neighborhoods it would come to me. Sure enough, it did. What was missing was landscaping. Now, the house being in the woods, what better landscaping could there be than Mother Nature herself. Well, Nancy loves to watch HGTV which has a show called Curb Appeal. So, hard as I tried, I lost the argument and we decided to hire someone to do landscaping around the house. As an Expressive, I had no patience to go line by line through the Yellow pages; I wanted a full-page screamingly colorful advertisement that appealed to someone like me, attracted to bright shiny objects. When I came across just such a page I invited the person to the house to give us an estimate for what he could do for us.

When the landscaper, Paul, arrived, there was something vaguely familiar about him. After a few minutes of conversation, I realized that he had actually attended one of my workshops on versatility several years earlier. I asked him if he had got anything out of it, since I, like many others in my profession, rarely get any feedback on the utility of the content. He said he found the content very useful to the point where using the versatility skills (the ability to communicate with others based on the other person's personality) had netted him an increase of 20% per year to his business. Needless to say, I was pleased with his comments. Then he said to me, "I'm going to come back in two days and give you a proposal for landscaping based on your personality." Man, I couldn't wait.

Two days later, Paul came to my house with three designs, each one colored in to match the different plantings and flowers he was planning on putting around the house. He said, "Don't look at these bare retaining walls. They'll be covered with ground cover flowing down like a river." I watched as he moved his hands down in an undulating fashion. In my mind I could see it. Then he said, "Don't look at these little bushes. In five years they will be these 15 foot rounds that you can carve into any shape you want." Again, I could see it in my mind because he was saying the words that Expressives want to hear (future orientation, multiple options). Then he said that all of this would die if I didn't get a sprinkler system. Since they didn't put those in, I would have to call a sprinkler system company.

When the sprinkler guy showed up, he talked about spread patterns and water usage, and how the sprinkler heads had just been re-engineered. He hauled me outside to show me a printout describing every single sprinkler head; it's spread pattern, range, design, and projected water use down to per head, per penny, per year. I can tell you that it was a good thing the landscaper was there because I was about to let my two German Shepherds loose on the sprinkler guy. Why? Because he was driving me nuts with the amount of detail he was providing. All I wanted to know is whether or not the sprinkler system would keep the landscaping from dying and would the cost fit with our budget. He, however, was meeting his own Analytical needs rather than my Expressive concerns. It was a toxic relationship.

Another toxic relationship is between Drivers and Amiables. Drivers will say, "You don't understand the business needs" while the Amiable will say, "Well, you don't understand the needs of the employees." Not quite as toxic as the Analytical/ Expressive exchange, but these people do tend to roll their eyes at each other out of disbelief.

A third toxic relationship that happens occasionally is between Drivers and Expressives because their orientations sometimes get in the way. Drivers are current timeframe, concrete, and planned. Expressives are future timeframe, spontaneous, and about as concrete as jello. When they are more flexible in their orientation, they get along fine.

If you want to find the most toxic relationship to you, look no further than your spouse … your first spouse. That's the opposites attract rule in action. Maybe at first there's an element of imagining you'll adapt to their way of being. However, the proof of the pudding is that soon they will be driving you crazy. If you believe you can change their basic personality, you're wrong, wrong, wrong. No, these kinds of relationships are pretty much doomed, and such pairs don't stay married unless one or both of them ups their versatility index sufficiently to meet the needs of the other person first.

I've already discussed the fact that self-diagnosis is not as accurate as the feedback you get from others. That's because we all tend to think we are better than we are, that we're all above average, and that we're all brilliant judges of character. True, we can be pretty on the ball when diagnosing others, but we're biased towards ignoring any negative characteristics about ourselves. So, while the diagnostic tool above provides you with a short quick way to figure out what you think you are, it would be better to have someone else who knows you well to make the call.

The compatible styles are:
- *Drivers and Analyticals*. Drivers provide the direction that Analyticals seek whilst Analyticals provide the data and details Drivers need to make better decisions.
- *Analyticals and Amiables*. Both are on the reactive side of the scale, reacting to the actions of others, though often in a passive-aggressive manner.

- *Amiables and Expressives*. They are both on the people side of the scale, as opposed to the task side where Analyticals and Drivers live.

Of course, people in the same style get along, except for Drivers with other Drivers. Think two bulls in a china shop. The way to get two Drivers to get along is to ask the question, "Who's responsible for what, by when, and how are we going to check with each other to make sure we're on the same track."

How do you overcome the toxic relationships? You actually have to increase your versatility, so you need some clues about how to do that. Versatility is based on a psychological concept called *interpersonal reciprocity*. Simply put, humans tend to give what they get. Most people think of this concept in the negative. If someone does something harmful to me or my family, my first instinct is to get even. This is the basic revenge pattern. But interpersonal reciprocity goes both ways. It's a two-edged sword; there's a positive side as well. If I do something that helps someone else, there is a strong unconscious desire to reciprocate, to help me in return. Helping others will trigger their inner desire to positively respond in kind. If I adjust my way of communicating to them in a way that meets their needs to receive information – based on their behavioral style, their personality – they are going to respond favorably and be helpful back.

The Key
So let's take a look at the overall key to unlocking the receptivity of each of the major behavioral styles:
- **Drivers** want to know *what* you are shooting for as outcomes – tasks and time frames.
- **Expressives** want to know *why*, for what future purpose, you are trying to accomplish these outcomes.
- **Amiables** want to know *who* is involved in the project, *whom* the information is collected from and to *whom* the

information will flow.

- **Analyticals** want to know *how* you plan on achieving the outcomes. What are the steps that will be taken to accomplish the goal.

Versatility with Drivers ...
Do:

- Be ready. Do 'completed staff work' ahead of time. Dot *I*s and cross *T*s.
- Be prepared to back up what you say.
- Organize your thoughts and presentations for speed. Keep it moving.
- Get to task immediately and stay on task. They probably don't care about your kids nor do they wish to tell you about theirs.
- Let them be in charge. Let them control how quickly or thoroughly you move through the material.
- End early whenever possible and leave quickly. Drivers like to save time.
- Whenever possible, let them "win." Present options, let them decide.
- Be clear, brief, and to the point.
- Stick to the business.
- Come prepared with all the requirements and objectives.
- Present the facts logically – plan for efficiency.
- Ask specific questions.
- Provide facts and figures about probability of success.
- If you disagree, take issue with the facts not the person.
- If you agree, support the results and the person.
- Persuade by referring to results.
- Leave when you're done.

Don't:

- Don't ramble or waste time.
- Don't try to build a personal relationship.
- Don't forget or lose things.
- Don't leave loopholes or cloudy issues.

- Don't ask rhetorical questions.
- Don't come with ready-made decisions.
- Don't speculate wildly or offer guarantees.
- If you disagree, don't let it reflect on them personally.
- If you agree, don't say "I'm with you."
- Don't try to convince by personal means.
- Don't direct or order.

With Expressives …
Do:

- Cut your material down to the high-level overview and present in a lively way. Spend extra time to add zip to your presentation.
- Follow their lead. Engage in socializing when they do. Go to what interests them in your material. Go with them on tangents and bring them back to task gently if you must.
- Think through what's in it for them and focus on that. What is the *why* for them?
- Involve them in a dialogue. Listen to them.
- Praise and support their idea.
- Provide the action plan and seek buy in.
- Support their dreams.
- Be stimulating.
- Leave time for relating and socializing.
- Ask their opinions.
- Provide ideas for action.
- Provide testimonials.
- Offer incentives.

Don't:

- Don't legislate.
- Don't kid around too much.
- Don't be curt, cold or tight-lipped.
- Don't do facts first.
- Don't deal with details.
- Don't leave things hanging in the air.
- Don't be impersonal or judgemental.

- Don't talk down to them.
- Don't be dogmatic.

With Amiables …
Do:
- Engage in small talk. Open up first to allow them to relax with you.
- Draw out their point of view. Listen and reflect their feelings.
- Clarify what is needed of them and offer your support.
- Work hard to maintain your franchise with them. Amiables want to like and be liked.
- Take a sincere interest in their hopes and concerns. Show that you care.
- Start with a personal comment.
- Show sincere interest in them.
- Draw out personal goals.
- Present your case softly.
- Ask *how* questions.
- Be casual and informal.
- Define individual contributions.
- Provide assurances and guarantees.

Don't:
- Don't rush into business.
- Don't stick to business.
- Don't be domineering or demanding.
- Don't debate about facts and figures.
- Don't manipulate or bully them.
- Don't patronize or demean them.
- Don't be abrupt or rapid.
- Don't be vague.
- Don't offer guarantees you can't deliver.

With Analyticals …

Do:

- Send the information package in advance to allow them processing time.
- Get to task; share a meeting agenda and follow it.
- Prepare thoroughly. Double-check all your facts. Organize your material to flow linearly and logically. Plug all the holes with hard data; anecdotes and personal opinions don't count with them.
- Present a balanced case. Present the negatives as well as the positives. Offer concrete strategies for minimizing the negatives.
- If they make a mistake, allow them to save face. They hate to be wrong or caught without information.
- Think through possible worst-case scenarios with them and develop contingency plans.
- Present realistic and detailed action plans and timelines.
- Approach them directly.
- Support their thoughtful approach.
- Take your time but be persistent.
- Draw up a step-by-step timetable.
- Give them time to think.
- Provide practical evidence.

Don't:

- Don't be disorganized.
- Don't be giddy or casual.
- Don't rush decisions.
- Don't be vague.
- Don't waste time.
- Don't provide personal incentives.
- Don't threaten, cajole, coax or whine.
- Don't use testimonials.
- Don't use opinions as evidence.
- Don't use gimmicks.

Do you recognize any of these in your life?

Do people vary according to the context – or are these deep determinants?

Circle All That Apply

Critical	Industrious	Pushy	Strong Willed
Indecisive	Persistent	Severe	Independent
Stuffy	Serious	Tough	Practical
Picky	Expecting	Dominating	Decisive
Moralistic	Orderly	Harsh	Efficient
Conforming	Supportive	Manipulating	Ambitious
Unsure	Respectful	Excitable	Stimulating
Ingratiating	Willing	Undiscipline	Enthusiastic
Dependent	Dependable	Reacting	Dramatic
Awkward	Agreeable	Egotistical	Friendly

Style Diagnostic Tool:
Count how many words you circled in each box.
The higher the number the more likely this style is yours.

Upper Left = Analytical	Upper Right = Driver
Lower Left = Amiable	Lower Right = Expressive

There can be combinations of styles.

Also notice if any of the boxes have nothing circled. When you look at those values, what is your response?

CHAPTER 7

Power Relationships

"Not everything that can be counted counts, and
not everything that counts can be counted."
~ ALBERT EINSTEIN

MONEY & POWER
Money is always a factor in every relationship.
Traditionally men are seen as the breadwinners,
and women the home-makers – although these distinctions
have been gradually disappearing over the last few decades.
Nowadays the Millennial generation are much more egalitarian,
less prejudiced, more sharing of roles. This is a trend that will
probably continue into the future, but even so, we are left with
the legacy of the 20th century views on marriage, family and
work relationships. Sugar-daddies and gold-diggers may still
exist, but only as a tiny minority.

Budgeting is a key activity in most long-term personal
relationships. However, profligate and secret spending by one
partner can easily give rise to mounting debt and relationship
discord, given the naive belief that putting things on a credit
card somehow doesn't count. Using plastic instead of notes and
coins makes a difference in how we experience spending money;
cards provide illusory power if they are not supported by actual
funds.

Even though in any well-functioning relationship the parties
usually do their best to keep things on an even keel, equality
is most unlikely. This imbalance in earning power or resources
may give rise to a sense of unfairness and disharmony. For
example, if the wife is earning more money than their partner,

she may resent the wastrel of a husband, the lower income earner. Why? They just do. "I've worked hard to get where I am" even though it may have been in a boring, demanding job, whereas the man has had what she considers an easy time engaging in more creative and fun activities which have not produced a regular income. Assessments are made of individual contributions – but this is often limited to how much money is coming in: "Look at what I'm doing for you?" This implies "you're not pulling your weight", despite the fact that you have just lost your job, or have spent months renovating the house, or whatever. It's the idea that the other person is sponging, getting something for nothing, whilst they are forced into the role of supporting the other person (who should be looking after themselves). If you measure personal worth in cash terms, you're in for a bumpy ride.

Status & Power

Status is an important quality of relationships. It's like we're all expert judges of relative status, and this ability is so common that we usually don't notice we're doing it. If we focus on one particular aspect of status – the power that we assign to people, and the actual power they have – and make a simple distinction about whether that person is *Strong or Weak*, and whether they tend to dominate in a relationship or are more compliant. This leads us to the key question: on this dimension, how well do people get along?

Strong–Strong

If you are both Strong, you tend to find a *mutually independent* based relationship. Both people are strong-willed, they know what they like and know how to get it. They don't want to waste time by being around people who appear indecisive. They are action-oriented, time sensitive, and organized. They like being challenged by other strong personalities with similar traits, just so long as their values are similar! One Strong personality may be taken aback when they meet another Strong – but once they realize they're able to get the job done together, they value their differences.

For example, take the political commentators Republican Mary Matalin and Democrat James Carval (LA Times, 2009). Both strong-willed, both highly opinionated, both challenging each other's ideas … to the betterment of both, but on opposite sides of the political spectrum. What makes their relationship work is the mutual respect each has for the other. Whilst they differ in their political orientation (one and one), they both hold similar solid values for the process of free political discourse found in the US political process. I'm sure, however, that during times of high political drama, they just agree to disagree. Strong-strong relationships require an appreciation for the other person's strength of conviction and character. Even strong people need support to thrive; no one thrives alone.

Weak–Strong

If one of the partners is weak, then you have a *dependent*-based relationship. Harry Levinson (a psychoanalyst at Harvard) once told me that no matter what position a person finds themselves in, they're there because they unconsciously want to be there; it's where they feel the safest. In a dependent-based relationship, the weaker person needs to be directed by (told what to do) by the stronger. That means the stronger person needs to be in charge and be able to give orders. As long as both parties feel their needs are being met, this relationship works. It doesn't work, however, if the stronger person takes advantage of what they perceive as subservience in the weaker partner. Then the relationship can turn abusive. Just because the weaker partner seeks the strength of the other to feel protected and safe, that does not give the stronger partner the right to negate their feelings or make them feel less worthy of love and respect.

Sometimes it's going to suit you to let other people be in charge – you're dependent upon their know-how and expertise – and you can learn something from them. You can let go of your need to be in control for a while and leave the decision-making to others. How long you can act out of character will depend on how important the situation is. For example, if you are on a guided tour of some landmark building, and this is part of a package deal, then, if you're not that interested in rococo architecture, given the chance you may prefer to goof off. However, if you're at a lecture and have to absorb the results of the latest research in a field you hope to make your name in, then you'd better pay attention. Your turn to be strong comes later, when you tell others what you've found out.

Weak–Weak

When both are weak, you have a *co-dependent, symbiotic* based relationship. This is where neither party wants to be in charge. Eventually, mostly out of momentum, decisions are made (see the Abilene Paradox in Chapter 23). No one wants to take charge for fear of upsetting the other. They feed off each other's indecision by supporting whatever behavior the other wants to engage in. As a result, bad behaviors tend to be encouraged because no one is strong enough to point out the negative aspects or consequences of what they are doing. This way you never learn, because there are never any good role models around. You get stuck in making poor judgments, especially of other people – as will be demonstrated in the bad dating choices you make: "I always seem to pick the wrong guys." Think Blake Edwards' (1962) *Days of Wine and Roses*. They need each other to survive; to put up with the behaviors no one else would. It's not very healthy in the long run, but it holds weak psyches together in the short term. They may realize they are hopeless cases but they do encourage each other to stay alive by offering comfort (see Banging on the Bus, Chapter 36).

Keeping a relationship on an even keel

How do you respond when something happens that is not to your liking, or doesn't happen when you think it should? For example, you're in a long-term relationship with someone

– a colleague or boss – and some agreement you have made in the past is not being upheld. There's nothing worse than unexplained silence – no phone calls, no emails, no tweets, nothing. Given that you have no idea what's happened, it's easy to become angry, aggressive or even vindictive. "How dare they ignore me!" you think, because to you that is a terrible thing in any relationship – it reduces your status to zero! So, before you fire off that angry tweet or email, just take a moment to think through the possible reasons. Maybe the other person is ill, or there's been an accident to them or to someone in their family. Did they go on vacation or trip at short notice and forget to tell you. Are they just overworked and don't have time to chat, because they have deadlines to meet? You get the picture – or at least, you can imagine several pictures which would explain what's happened.

The need for closure

Incompleteness tends to make us nervous. Generally speaking, we like to live in a world which is predictable, secure, knowable. We want everything neat and tidy, no gaps. We are uncomfortable with loose ends: we fret over items that have gone missing; we don't like unsolved mysteries, because we want to know what happens in the end and can't relax until we achieve closure. However, when we find information is missing, we fill the gaps by making stuff up. But we don't necessarily fill in these blanks with positive information, but with negatives. Imagining what might go wrong is a self-protection mechanism; it keeps us from getting hurt. So, if we're in the dark, we tend to think worst-case scenarios. The boss calls you into their office but doesn't tell you why. What's the first thing you think of when your boss says to you, "Carl, I'd like to see you in my office." It's like being called to the principal's office at school. "What did I do now?"! Or your significant other doesn't pick up your call so you think that they're trying to hide something from you or that they are hurt or even dead. Or you're waiting for someone to arrive, and however many times you look at the clock, they're not there. Until suddenly they are. Now you're never going to get back those wasted minutes. So take a deep breath, and instead of berating them for tardiness, be glad that they have actually arrived. Be pleased to see them; simply forget the time before, because truth be told, you're probably more annoyed by the fact that you hadn't planned on the delay, and didn't have anything to occupy you. So "Hi! How are you?" with a smile. Remember that everyone has a background life to which you are not party, and which influences the bit of their life that you witness.

Being aggressive is not usually a good option; it's not always about you. And whatever is going on in someone else's life may be none of your business. The best solution is to start out with honest neutrality. If you don't know something, or what is going on, tell yourself "I don't know. Could be good, could be bad. I'll have to wait and see." Every time you then find yourself thinking negative thoughts, say that mantra over to yourself. You may just have to be patient. If you are desperate to fill in the blanks with actual facts then you'll have to do some research, explore further avenues. Be humble. Go in low status, show concern "I'm worried in case there's something wrong." This is about how you feel, not about blaming them. That way you are more likely to understand things from their point of view. They probably weren't deliberately trying to annoy you; it was just that something happened that got in the way of your relationship. Then "So what can I do to help?" or "Is there any way in which I can assist you?" Be prepared for a No. Otherwise, you could ask, "So what is one thing I could to do move things forward?" which will flip them out of their stuff and see things from a wider perspective.

Bigger, Better, Further, Faster ...
Another human tendency in groups is to try to raise your status by boasting or bragging. Some people always want to appear higher status than you – whatever your expertise, they know

that little bit more. Your auto? Theirs is "top of the range – you wouldn't believe how much it cost!" Vacation? They went further on the dream holiday of a lifetime around the world, when you just managed Orlando. "Florida is so *passé*" they say. Although it's meant kindly, people keep asking, "Where are you going on vacation this year?" They might want to know, so that they can then show their superior knowledge of the area, or region, or country. And it is so easy to fall into this way of talking. Someone mentions Italy, and you want to tell them about your holiday in Tuscany, or Venice and then to add disparaging remarks about the other 'tourists' or the sun being too hot or the streets full of water. Same thing with restaurants or disasters that happened to you. The list is endless.

What they claim may be true, but it doesn't advance the relationship very much. For them, everything is bigger and brighter, and they will talk about their lives in such a way as to suggest that they are superior and you are completely out of their league. You feel that whatever they do or say is going to be some kind of put-down. They may not realize they are doing this. It's probably not much use drawing attention to this either, as they will be unable to absorb this information in the way you would like them to, and merely see this as a further sign of your inferiority: "You're just envious", "Are you complaining? Get over it." They defend themselves well.

You have to consider: does it really matter to me that they are playing this game? If you allow it to make you feel bad, there is not much you can do other than walk away. If you spot these symptoms in another person, accept that they have this condition and try to use it positively. Ask them for their opinion, how they would do things, how they would solve the problem. You'll be able to recognize good answers as well as the bullshit. Whatever you get, thank them for their suggestion. You'll know what to do with it.

So are you going to own up to playing this *Better than you* game yourself? Surely not. That car you just bought – did you really need to go for the latest model? That story you told about the hotel in Tuscany – are you sure it happened like that, or did you add a few flourishes for effect to make you look good? In the stories we tell, some of the facts are going to get a bit distorted, the events enhanced to bring out the key points we want to get across. We will downplay those aspects of the situation which show us in a poor light – because there's nothing wrong with bending the facts just a little – if it leads to a better story.

The Halo Effect

Part of the reason for doing this is that we think it will reflect on us, enhance our status, and at the same time, shine up our halo. There is a well-studied phenomenon known as the Halo Effect. What that means is that we tend to connect one quality to another – if someone is attractive then they must be intelligent – that sort of thing, even though there is no actual connection between them.

This kind of thinking is particular rife in business. If a company is doing well, sales and profits are high, then we assume that the CEO is some kind of genius or visionary leader. Yes, we're very good at general impressions – it's our way of knowing how to act fast – but the problem is we then take that as a truth and draw conclusions from it which are not supported. That leads to thinking that we have discovered the magic formula for excellence: "We just have to do what Company X did, and we, too, will be showered with financial success." The trouble is, it doesn't work like that. We've made too many connections which are unjustified or plain false. It's a hard fact to swallow, but a great deal of business success is essentially random, based on chance happenings. We make up stories based on cause and effect, even though we don't understand what's really going on. The more complex our business is – consider the myriad factors out of our control which affect world markets – the more we are blowing in the wind. Some companies are lucky and get a windfall. Others muddle along, doing much the same thing, keeping steady as she goes.

So is this why we would like to mingle with the great and the good, to snap a selfie standing next to a star? We think their glamor will somehow transfer across to us? Well, maybe their charisma will actually give us a boost. Because we want stars, we want heroes, we want magic formulas for success. Alas, there are no short-cuts, no guaranteed solutions to all the problems and issues we are likely to encounter. What matters is learning from experience – ours and other people's – and practicing what to do ahead of time, so that when something happens, you can deal with it. This is common with firefighters, airline pilots, war correspondents, and all those who put themselves in positions of trust and potential danger. There is no reason why we all shouldn't use the stories of others, to build our own repertoire of Things to do when x happens.

CHAPTER 8
Interesting relationships

Fuel for the Relationship Fire

> Having lit the fire of relationship, we managed to keep it
> going for a while, but lacking the correct fuel, we let the
> fire go out. Now we stir the ashes, wondering what went
> wrong. But whatever we decide now, it's too late. No
> amount of bellows work is going to rekindle this one.

'INTERESTING' IS AN INTERESTING WORD – it's rather vague,
and yet we easily apply it to other people. *Interesting*
suggests that they do something we do not do ourselves
– for example, they have spent years living in remote places, or
have achieved fame with their music or artistic talent, or talk
and act in a way which is not the norm within your local group.
Interesting says that there is more to them, and that intrigues us
because what we see is just the surface. It suggests a mystery
because not all is revealed. Essentially, you want to know more;
you would like to spend more time with interesting people.

Look in the mirror and without putting yourself down, consider,
"What makes me interesting?" If you hold the belief that
everyone is interesting in their own way, because we have all
lived different lives, then you have the basis for exploring any
relationship. When we think about ourselves, we tend to dismiss
the idea of being interesting because it's just little ol' me, the me
I've grown up with, and treat as ordinary – simply because you
have accepted the things that you've done: "Doesn't everyone
do this?" No, they don't. Not everyone has built shelters for
earthquake victims or helped in a hospital in a third world
country. At the same time, not everyone has spent years working
in a clothing retail outlet, or behind the bar in a down-town pub.
We have all had experience of being special at some time – if

only we remember to check it out, to go beneath the surface and identify what it was that brought out the best in you.

Apply this to everyone you meet. Assume they have had interesting and unique experiences. Trouble is, they think they're rather boring or ordinary, so that means you have to winkle out this kind of information. I once asked a rather elderly and irritatingly fussy lady, who had once been a top ballet-dancer, which had been her most memorable performance. "Performing *Swan Lake* before an audience of Australian miners at the Broken Hill steel works." Now that conjures up an interesting image!

An essential part of building good relationships is sharing personal details. However much people tell about themselves, this can only ever be the tip of the iceberg. You could treat the things they tell you as cues – opportunities for you to ask them more, go deeper, find out more about this aspect or event in their life. People are naturally experts on themselves, and given the chance enjoy talking about themselves (don't you?). However, they often get stuck in grooves, telling the same old stories over and over, and probably boring themselves in the process. So go beyond the usual. Instead of just swapping stories or talking about yourself, ask *them* questions, because there are plenty of things you don't yet know about the other person's past, or how they will deal with something upcoming. Be curious and frame your questions by "Tell me more about the time you …" or "What was the most exciting/fearful/embarrassing/bizarre … experience you had." So while you're showing an interest, you're boosting their ego, and building a stronger bond between you. It may or may not go anywhere, because sharing our lives with others is a voluntary act, and we never quite know what is going to happen next, nor how the other person will react to us. Be genuinely curious about them and their life – within reason. They'll let you know if you're going too far.

Asking Why questions

Very young children soon learn the trick of asking Why
questions, and they'll push it, and you, to the limit. You are
expected to know the answer to everything! And they will not
be satisfied with dismissive answers. There has to be an ultimate
reason, doesn't there? Well, who knows? But we're good at
making up stories and answers to most things, hoping that they
will suffice for the inquiring minds of others. So over time, do
we become just a little defensive when others ask us Why …?
"Why did you marry that person?" "Why don't you want to join
our group?" and so on.

Sometimes you may be pushing it when you want people to
explain why they did what they did, or how they reached a
particular decision or conclusion, especially when clarifying the
thinking behind a decision being made. At times people are not
sure themselves; are you always clear why you did things, or did
not do things?

It seems reasonable to assume that if a decision has been made,
then there will have been some reasoned justification. If the
other person finds this hard to put into words, then come at this
from another angle. For example, ask about their intention:
- What were you hoping to achieve?
- How did you want things to be different?
- What was the problem you were trying to solve?
- What would have happened if you hadn't done that?

Of course, you may want to soften your questions, with "I'm
curious …" "I've been wondering …"

Overcoming Boredom

Sometimes you get to the point when you think you've heard
everything you want to know about that other person. You've sat
through their stories many times, and you could possibly repeat
them yourself. So what's new? That's your challenge. Is it worth
trying to go beyond the façade they present to the world? Or do

you just be polite?

If that other person is your long-term partner, what then? Or to put it bluntly, is your marriage getting into a rut? And how much does that reflect upon you? After all, when you notice that's happening, you're also running in the same groove. How long have you been doing that?

Is it time to sit down together and decide what you can possibly do to revitalize your relationship? Make an appointment, and, in the intervening time, look widely for ideas. Including all those plans you made earlier in your life about what you wanted to do but never did.

Then, when you are together, explore each other's failed dreams in order to see what would still work. Essentially you're looking for projects that focus the mind, not on the relationship but on things that are challenging and which you could do together. And as a contingency plan, those things you could do separately, but which would make you and your relationship more interesting. What else could you bring to the table that you could share?

Run this discussion along the lines of a brainstorming session. That is, you set the theme, each work independently jotting down ideas – the more the merrier – and then share the ideas without dismissing anything as impracticable at this stage. The aim is to stimulate ideas; your brain does not need more practice in demolishing someone else's. Entertain possibilities and variations of possibilities. And then choose a direction and work out the first step. What is one thing you can do to start that project? The first step. Put a time limit on it. Do it soon, while your enthusiasm is high.

Creative Partnerships
Some of the most interesting and inspiring relationships give rise

to a creative explosion of ideas. A couple of people bounce ideas off each other and the result is an outstanding achievement, far superior to anything they could have done on their own. The whole is greater than the sum of the parts. When you find a partner like this, treasure them.

Recall some well-known creative partnerships:
Computers: Steve Jobs and Steve Wozniak
Movies: Joel and Ethan Coen, the Farrelly Brothers, the Wachowski brothers
Music: John Lennon & Paul McCartney; Paul Simon and Art Garfunkel; Jerry Leiber and Mike Stoller
Dance: Fred Astaire and Ginger Rogers, and so on.

It's a case of having someone around who thinks along similar lines to you, but is just that bit different so that they flip you into different grooves in your thinking. As you go along with the new idea, rather than immediately negating it, you will discover much more that shines a new light on your project. Each person in a creative partnership contributes a blending of skills; each has an appreciation of what the other person brings to the relationship.

So how can we make such situations more likely to occur. For a start, we need to be unafraid to explore where no one has gone before. We need to say Yes to new ideas, rather than rejecting them because they were 'not invented here' (a phrase that still occurs in some businesses, where personal ownership of ideas is more important than finding new products or ways to market).

It's not about fame; it's about having fun, going with the flow, seeing where you get to. It's about supporting the other person, respecting their contributions. There will be loads of ideas that don't hit the mark, have no commercial potential, or are kind of irrelevant to your current lifestyle. The point is, by having a huge number of ideas, you can choose the best. If you only have one idea, and it doesn't work, you're left with nothing.

The key factor here is your attitude, your willingness to learn, explore, be curious and not worry that much of what you do will be seen by others as mistakes or plain nonsense. The aim is not to become famous as a result; it is to fulfill your potential. You're tuning in to the way people naturally grow and develop, and achieving mastery at doing whatever it is. The unfortunate thing is that you probably had a lot of this knocked out of you at school. In your teen years it became uncool to do certain things, such as think creatively because that upset the teachers whose primary aim was to keep to the timetable. Wild ideas were not on the agenda. As a result, you learned to keep your ideas to yourself; you became deliberately uncreative. Do not despair; there is a remedy, and it's not too late.

Curiosity

> "The flame of curiosity doesn't burn in a vacuum."
> ~ IAN LESLIE, *Curious: The Desire to Know and Why Your Future Depends on It* (2014:187)

Curiosity needs encouragement. It has become a common belief that children start out curious, but during their school years this curiosity is somehow dissipated. This may be true to the extent that natural curiosity gets in the way of teaching a core curriculum. The more you know, the more questions arise about the world: What else? What if? Tell me more. And this is the time when the question is a constant "Why?" How do you answer these questions? It's a tough balance between imparting facts and maintaining a good level of wanting to know. If you give too much information, then curiosity can be swamped; children soon learn that they can find out stuff on the internet. If you fail to give encouragement, the children learn that their excitement is wasted on you. If it's a case of too much or too little, people give up.

So now, in your adult life, where do you stand on being curious? Were you told it was not polite to ask questions? Standards were different in your parents' time. Could you dig out those questions you always wanted to ask but were afraid to have social displeasure heaped on you? Can you believe it is now safe to do so, and that the consequences will be life enhancing? It's also worth remembering that other people may be in the same boat – with things they were always wondering about, but never got clear. So by asking questions you're also doing them a favor. It's a good idea to frame questions with a disarming statement about yourself: "I'm curious. Can you tell me about the time you said you worked in a department store?" or "I've often wondered, why did you give up teaching?"

A word of warning. Treat the information you receive as confidential regardless of how trivial it seems. It's not fuel for gossip. It's their stuff, so unless the other person expressly states that it's for public consumption or talks about it openly, keep it to yourself.

CHAPTER 9
Context and Behavior

MAYBE IT'S NO ONE'S FAULT. It's so easy to blame other people for their supposed traits or their dysfunctional behavior (to your eyes – because it's never you that's creating the disturbance!). But there could be another factor here: the actual context, the space you find yourselves in. Critical factors could include all of Herzberg's Hygiene factors, and that includes the lighting (too dark or too bright, type of lighting: daylight or fluorescent); the heating (too hot or too cold); noise levels (not easy to concentrate when jackhammers are nearby); the room itself (does it have windows?), the office layout (cubicle or open-plan), ease of movement (free passage or clutter in the way); as well as the furniture, the architecture and design features. All these factors affect behavior to some extent. For example, in low light or darkness, people do things they wouldn't do in broad daylight. Color, also, can affect people's behavior. Some colors are calming, others exciting. For example, some prisons have been painted bright pink in order to have a calming effect (see Alter, 2013).

The rationale here is that when you notice how the world impinges on you, you'll have a better understanding of how it affects others. Not precisely, but you'll learn to ask the right questions and be able to adjust your living and working spaces. By paying attention to the environment, and by removing anything that gets in the way, you can subtly enhance everyone's experience by ensuring you have optimal conditions for what you want to do.

There are many subtle influences around us which we are not aware of. Some of these may be key factors that affect our and others' behavior. Some you can pick up on by looking. For example, the arrangement of furniture. Does your rest area resemble the waiting area at an airport or the snug alcove in your favorite restaurant? I once worked in a newly built psychology department where the staffroom – a large square space – had all the chairs pushed to the walls, presumably to make it easier for the cleaning people to do their job. Few people would hang around once they'd had their coffee. A simple rearrangement – putting the chairs in clusters, close enough so that people could chat facing each other – made a huge difference. Suddenly this room became alive with conversation. People now sat in groups and stayed to talk to each other. The key factor here was that I noticed this and physically shifted the furniture around myself when no one was looking! I was conducting an experiment. Otherwise, inertia rules; people will tolerate suboptimal conditions if they are not too bad.

So how about designing space to make it easy for people to do what you want them to do? After all, that's what supermarkets do with their designs – you have to walk through most of the store to find the everyday essentials, which means passing by all the other non-essentials they'd like you to buy. One thing worth noticing is that there is a space just inside the store, where people stop and reorient – you could say, go into shopping trance mode. They enter through the door and then they stop – which is not so good for people coming in behind them. So be aware of these transition spaces. Make sure they are kept clear, and make the next space inviting so that people move forward rather than cause a blockage.

Context affects your behavior in that you have learned to behave appropriately depending on where you are. Think for a moment about the meaning of spaces. How do you feel when you enter:
  • An hotel; a conference center; a sports arena.
  • An art gallery; restaurant; elevator.
  • A masonic lodge or the inner sanctum of some esoteric organization.

- A cathedral, a church, temple or synagogue, or the religious sanctum of a different religion or culture.
- A supermarket or shopping mall.
- On stage at a theatre or conference center.
- Your boss's office; your own house.

Each of these places has different rules and expectations. Of course, you may choose to violate the norms and suffer the consequences. But then, by pushing the boundaries, you may find that the boundary is elastic and that others will be grateful to you for pointing this out.

This applies not just to buildings; people have their own personal space around them. They have a preferred distance at which they keep away from others. Some warm cultures like to get in close; those of a cooler culture find this intrusive so they back off. The degree of intimacy you have with another person will be reflected in how much of their personal space they will let you into. At first, you stay at hand-shake distance. Only very good friends and lovers enjoy very close approaches and contact.

The power of furniture

If you want to maintain your higher status, make sure that you have the boss chair and everyone else is physically lower than you. And while you're at it, make sure your back is to the window so that it's hard for them to see you against the light.

If you are at a meeting, consider the difference having a table makes. The table not only provides a practical surface for writing, it also forms a physical barrier that protects you to some extent. The shape of the table, and who sits where also give a subtle message. If you go the King Arthur route, and treat people as equals (more or less), then the round table is for you. If you want to maintain differences, rectangular will do this. Choose where to sit: do you sit at the end of the long table, or in the middle of the longer side? It will affect how you come across and how connected the other people will feel. And who do you want sitting on your right hand …?

When you are meeting people for the first time it's often a good idea to choose a neutral place – an away venue for all parties. A restaurant or café gives no one the initial advantage. Then, as the meeting progresses and behaviors and status are revealed, you'll get the lay of the land, the relative status of all participants – information to be used with discretion in further encounters.

CHAPTER 10
Status

"A comedian is someone paid to lower his own or
other people's status."
~ KEITH JOHNSTONE, *Impro*, p. 39

ALL HUMAN GROUPS DEVELOP HIERARCHIES based on relative
status – pretty much in the same way that birds and
animals do. For example, you find alpha males in each
pride of lions, and a pecking order in each flock of chickens.
Because this way of sorting ourselves is natural, much of the
time we don't notice we're doing it. But when someone comes
across as putting on airs and graces or suddenly starts to talk
posh or act superior, you suffer momentary surprise or your
hackles rise: you're ready to do combat to defend your position!
Just like in the animal kingdom, it's easy to get into fights to
establish dominance. We may not do it with fists or wrestling,
but there are many ways in which we tussle for power, in order
to be top dog or to keep up with the neighbors.

We know from personal experience where we lie on the power
or dominance scale. It's usually quite easy to place other people
according to whether they are above you or below you. Status
is not fixed, but varies according to context and purpose. When
you are part of a social group, people often take it in turns to be
in control and to be controlled; your relative position goes up a
bit and down a bit. Over a period your status kind of averages
out. This makes for groups in which for much of the time we're
getting along nicely, thank you. Groups function well when
everyone knows their place.

When we encounter people we don't know, even as they appear in the distance, we are calculating relative status. We gather a general impression and much of the time we're pretty accurate. That means we know how to behave with them. We notice the way they move, the way they talk, what they look at, and how they're dressed. What they are wearing is often a real giveaway.

Eyes are important. "Look me in the eye and say that" is a challenge to someone's status. Are you going to stare them down? To avoid being lowered, for example, police officers (who have high status, and coercive power conferred by their uniform) make sure you can't see their eyes by shielding them with dark mirror glasses.

Direct eye-to-eye contact is very leveling. It's a way of minimizing status differences. It starts with smiling – genuine smiling, which involves the muscles around the eyes. False smiling doesn't do that, and we can tell the difference. You can tell a lot from someone else's eyes; for example, are they in the here and now, or lost in some distant internal state? Are they interested in you, or are their eyes darting around the room looking for escape? But if they are open to you, it's as if you're entering a shared reality, making genuine contact. If you are not used to making eye-contact, then task yourself to do it for the next dozen or so people you meet. Rather than a hard stare, use soft eyes by relaxing the muscles around your eyes. Cue yourself up to remember, because it's just too easy to fall back into habits of avoidance and self-protection. Don't stare, just look at them and think how you could compliment them – but rather than saying anything, smile and say hello in whatever way's appropriate.

We are sometimes fooled when someone is deliberately trying to act higher (looking down their nose at you) or lower (looking up at you) in order to gain some advantage. Give yourself the air of authority, put on a business suit or wear a white coat, and you'll find it easier to get other people to do what you want. It could be a con, or it could just be a short cut through red tape. Act like a boss and people will clear a path before you. When we meet someone who gives off this sense of personal power, we feel intimidated or inferior – or grateful that someone seems to know what they are doing. We show our low status by bowing and scraping, tugging a forelock, and calling them Sir or Ma'am. Isn't that, after all, how you react (on the inside, at least) in the boss's presence? It's possible to bring them down to a more level playing field by seeing through their pretense, looking them in the eye, and agreeing politely with what they say.

When you are in the presence of someone with authority, for example, the boss, the head teacher, the president, the *ex officio* person – police, security guard, and so on, they expect you to obey their requests or demands. If you don't they tend to switch off their personal relationship, and resort to officialdom – invoking the rules, the law, the regulations.

The way you speak, and the words you use – especially in a status- and class-obsessed society like the UK – will immediately let others know where you stand. A prime example would be with the royal family, and the pomp and pageantry that goes with them. In many societies, we collectively confer high status on a particular family – Presidents, State Governors, Foreign dignitaries, movie-stars and other high fliers – and we, so to speak, treat them like royalty. No red carpet is long enough.

If you want to work together on something in a team, then, to avoid a clash of wills or status, shift your position so that you are not directly in front of them – that's an aggressive stance – you will literally and metaphorically get on their side by standing beside them. Then you can position the topic of discussion in that vague space out in front of you which you indicate with your hands.

Adjust your status

Within the group or team, there is going to be a level in which you are most comfortable. But this will vary, so it's a good idea to be flexible and adapt to other people. You don't need lessons in this. You're frequently doing this to some degree with the range of people you meet. The only difference is that you're now aware that you're doing it. So if you're expected to raise your status, like you're suddenly promoted to leader or expert, then adjust your breathing, your posture, the way you look at the other people, so that you take on the familiar mannerisms of the people you know who have such a status. It also helps to move to a new position. This gives you time to take on your high status. When you reach the spot – the head of the table, the podium, wherever – pause … look at the other people, let your breath out, and relax into your new role. You're ready to go.

Once you know your place, you have a starting point for communicating to others. Pitch your communication at an appropriate level which they feel comfortable with. Once you've established this neutral ground, you can try raising your status to challenge the other person or to get them to comply. Again, we're doing this anyway; what you need is to notice what's going on and to monitor how they respond. It's a good idea to position yourself just a bit above or just a bit below; this will give you a negotiating advantage. If you want to provoke a reaction from them, then exaggerate. Go very high "I don't think much of your behavior. I think you should seriously consider your position."

So if raising your status – acting tough, in control, superior – creates tension in other people, then doing the opposite, lowering your status, can be used to defuse a situation. How do you do that? Play dumb. Any kind of helplessness would do. But don't overdo it unless the situation calls for a comedy act. For example, the ultimate ruse is to imitate an animal victim by falling on the floor and exposing your vulnerable part – your neck – which makes the attacker stop. But that really is a final resort. Better to look a bit puzzled, and act or own up to being ignorant, by asking (sensible) questions, "Forgive me, could you explain that bit again?" If you reveal that "I've never really understood …" then within a group you'll probably find others with the same problem but who have not been brave enough to ask.

CHAPTER 11

Expectations

A woman goes to see a Private Investigator. She tells him that she thinks her husband is having an affair, and that she would like to know the truth.

GIVEN THIS FAMILIAR SCENARIO, CONSIDER: What happens next? When you have thought through some possible consequences, mentally step back and think about how you did that, what happens in your mind as you use your imagination. You will have probably made sense of the words by thinking up some images: a room, two people talking, a sign on the door perhaps – that will have been influenced by your previous experience (often second-hand, and gained through books, movies or TV shows). And you can probably continue the story based on 'what usually happens next' and because of your familiarity with the Private Detective scenario, you can predict what is likely to happen next.

For example, if you are acquainted with the works of Agatha Christie or Raymond Chandler, or if you have seen the movies with Humphrey Bogart, such as *The Maltese Falcon* or *In a Lonely Place,* then you know that there will be an investigation, in which other information is revealed that provides a complex understanding of the motivations and desires of the characters involved. However, the path to the solution may not be straightforward. We could be mistaken (or deliberately misled) into thinking that what we see at first is the truth or is the real mystery to be solved. For example, in the 1974 movie *Chinatown*, the story starts as above, but later we realize that something very different is going on. Perhaps we are alerted at the beginning of *Chinatown* by the way that the Private Investigator, Jake Gittes (played by Jack Nicholson) says to the woman:

> "Do you love your husband? Then go home and
> forget all about it. … I'm sure that he loves you
> too. … Do you know the expression, Let sleeping
> dogs lie? You're better off not knowing."
> (Towne, 1974, 1998: 8)

This response is unexpected. When you watch the movie, it is actually quite shocking. You do not expect a Private Investigator to say this. And what he says has some deep implications, reflecting on the nature of relationships, and so on. If this were a real life situation, the woman would then have to reconsider what she would actually do. Her expectations have changed, simply as the result of hearing some words from another person. As audience/observer, you may also have modified your own ideas on how to respond to such situations.

This is one secret about relationships: people behave in unexpected ways; you cannot rely on the past to predict the future. People change. Yes, they really do, despite any efforts to prevent it happening. You change; boredom works as an incentive. Fashion and technology also introduce the element of updating yourself. So, if you want to keep a relationship vibrant and growing, include a number of surprises, do things that the other person does not expect. That's why you need to practice ways of thinking differently and finding the right words that will help other people change their perception of whatever their current situation is.

Living in Ambivalence

> It's not too hard to imagine
> That I never left the country
> But stayed home, married the girl,
> And never saw the Southern Cross,
> while floating at midnight
> in the swimming pool.

In practical terms, each of us has to learn to deal with the conflicting pulls of certainty and uncertainty. We both need to define the world, to know things, who we are, how it all works, and at the same time, be able to express our creativity, to be curious, to upset things, to explore the unknown and enjoy the surprises the future brings. In personal terms, we want to find *the* answer (to life, the universe and everything) and yet we are still wondering what questions to ask, or contemplating "What if I were to ...?" Being authentic means accepting rather than resisting these two pulls and learning to balance them. Being a sham is pretending that one of them doesn't exist. (Would you like me to tell you your future? I see a major change in your life approaching. It's not without its difficulties, but you will overcome them ...). We leave a trail behind us, but the path into the future is as yet untrodden.

Living with this awareness of uncertainty can be tough at times, so we seek diversions. We spend much of our lives not living in the here and now but in some made-up past or future, or in some alternate reality that has been generated in the lands created by various media. Sometimes we relive our decisions, and wonder "What if I had done X instead of Y..." and then feel emotional about different outcomes. The future may turn out very much like the past. If it didn't, everyday life would be really challenging. We use our accumulated stories and scenarios to predict what is likely to happen. This works, much of the time – except when it doesn't. Expect the unexpected, as the saying goes.

How do you live with ambivalence? It's easy. You've been doing it all your life, without realizing it. You have an understanding of the world that seems solid and real. It's how things are. It works in terms of cooking dinners, or catching buses to work. It's dependable, to an extent. Well, at least the sidewalk stays firm under your feet. Until the day it doesn't and collapses, but never mind. We treat the everyday world as real. But we also know that everything is changing, to some degree, all the time. Think about what was on your plot of land a century ago? How did you ever manage before computers and the internet? How did you contact people without a cell-phone? Remember VHS video-recorders and cameras that used 35mm film? Perhaps the only thing that hasn't changed are the programs on TV!

Many of the frustrations of life arise because of the failure of our expectations. We think we know what will happen, how other people will behave, how things ought to be – but we are often wrong. If things threaten us (because we have not prepared for them) the usual response is to say No, to negate, to refuse offers and reject opportunities. If we have strong feelings about what happens, if our basic beliefs are threatened, then we may go into denial or fail to cope rather than accept them. Maintaining several conflicting beliefs at once can be confusing, stressful, and debilitating. Therefore it's a good idea to step back and notice what you're doing, where the discrepancies arise with other person's view of the world. How are they seeing things differently? What do they see which you do not? What do you see that they don't? Here you have either the basis of conflict or the springboard for exploration and creativity.

Are you able to let go of old expectations that were not fulfilled? "Oh, got that wrong." Or do you hang on to ideas simply because you had them, and they fitted the world you wanted to bring into being? Some people do this with failed relationships. Even though the evidence is plainly in front of them – your girl has chosen to be with someone else, not you – you think you can make the relationship work? Dream on. If you ever find yourself in such a situation, take a moment to notice the rules, the oughts you have applied, to realize what you are *not* seeing. Again, the folk wisdom tells us: You can't win 'em all. In a practical sense, we need to practice staying open to events, of being curious about our perceptions, which means keeping your options open, rather than denying what is obvious to everyone else. It's time to move on.

CHAPTER 12
Health Benefits

IN HER BOOK, *THE VILLAGE Effect*, Susan Pinker explains how important it is to have frequent face-to-face contact with one another. In France (and Europe in general), this is literally true. French people greet each other with not just handshakes (for the men) but with 'kisses' (*bisous*) on both cheeks. Loudness can be a factor: *Mwaah*! You are expected to greet people you know well this way the first time you encounter them each day. If you attend any kind of meeting, you are expected to at least shake hands with everyone else. If you are in a public place, such as the post-office where people are waiting to be served, you also greet them verbally. This is probably not the norm in urban settings in the UK or US.

So how do we include touch in our communication without feeling embarrassed? Women tend to have fewer problems with this, but men often do. They substitute sensitivity with heartiness – slapping each other on the shoulder or punching somewhere in the upper body or arm. Even the bear hug can come over as false if the body behind it is tense and uptight. Somehow, it's seen as unmanly to make genuine contact – as evidenced by a nervous laugh or a joke that is intended to defuse the power of touching.

All this touchy-feely stuff not only includes you in the local community – you feel as though you belong there to some extent (if you weren't born there, you will never completely belong, and will always be seen by the natives as an outsider to some degree) – but is actually good for your health. The physical contact is good for our cardiovascular and immune systems:

> "… the right kind of social contact (hostility doesn't work) instructs the body to secrete more endogenous opiates, which act as local painkillers, and fewer hormones such as adrenaline, noradrenaline, and corticosteroids— the body's often destructive answer to immediate stressors—which can wage an ongoing war on our tissues and our physical resilience."
> ~ PINKER (2015:21)

In cultures where touch is part of the way you do things, it's done unselfconsciously. However, when Americans or Brits try to emulate these other cultures, they are slightly embarrassed and self-conscious and so make a comment about it, which suggests they are not actually enjoying the physical touch and not getting the oxytocin benefit. Mutually acceptable touch releases oxytocin which makes us feel good. However, if people are confused and anxious about what they should do, this raises the opposite of oxytocin which is cortisol.

So are you going to deliberately up your oxytocin levels by hugging everyone? Be careful. It's one thing for the man to hug the woman, and feels he's getting something nice out of it, but the woman can experience quite controlling behavior so in that case it is not a nice thing to have done to you. There has to be a look that says, "We both want this."

You can learn a lot about another person by touching them – all you need is the minimum contact – their hand will do. Anyone who has done any martial arts training will confirm this. It's a matter of paying attention to something most of us ignore. As you increase your sensitivity, the more you can 'know' about the other person's state – how tense they are, for sure, how balanced they are.

There's a lot you can tell from a handshake. You may have suffered the iron-grip of someone who thinks it's a good idea to crush your hand-bones. It hurts; it's not friendly. How do you tell people not to do that? Well, you could shake your hand in the air to loosen it up again, nurse it in your armpit and engage in some heavy panting, or collapse bodily and fall in a heap on the floor – that might get the message across. But the thing is, if they are as insensitive as to want to crush you in the first place, then they might be kind of impervious to the feedback they are getting. Fist-bump, anyone?

Psychologists have conducted several experiments to find out the effects of light non-sexual touch – such as a one-second touch on the arm, or brief contact with the other person's hand when they give you something or hand you your change. In a restaurant situation, people will often give a bigger tip to a waitress who has touched them (Crusco & Wetzel, 1984). Although the response to touching can vary according to the culture – think of the Mediterranean temperament – people generally come across as friendlier, more likely to comply with your wishes, honest, agreeable, when appropriately touched. It's also true that people of higher status (see Chapter 10) tend to touch more than those with less power.

> Touch communicates something vital about power relationships. Henley (1973) observed people in a major city as they went about their daily business. The people who tended to touch others (versus those being touched) were usually higher status. Generally we regard people who touch others as having more power in society (Summerhayes & Suchner, 1978).

How big a stretch would it be to find opportunities for touching other people a bit more? You do it with your loved ones – spouse, children, parents – so how could you extend this to a wider circle of friends? Imagine them as part of your family? Perhaps it would be easier to lighten the load if you are a bit of a back-slapper. Your sexuality is not being challenged. Just be more friendly, with a light touch. Aim for the arm – that's usually a safe area for most people. Use this kind of touch as an accompaniment to sharing of personal stuff. Touch the arm lightly as you say "You know, I've always appreciated what you did …"

You will no doubt encounter people who shy away at the perceived threat of being touched. That's their choice, based on some aspect of fear. There's probably not much you can do about this. Just respect their preference and accept the limp, lifeless handshake as a statement of where they are at. Match the level of intensity and move on to more important things.

CHAPTER 13

Do You Live to Eat or Eat to Live?

"Eat to live, don't live to eat."
~ BENJAMIN FRANKLIN

CULTURAL CONNECTIONS
Formality has its rituals, and in certain cultures, it is expected that you will act in a respectful way. That means going along with the other person's traditional ways of doing things. It's not about giving in or complying in a demeaning way – it's greasing the wheels of the relationship. For example, the Japanese bow to each other much more than people in the West do. It's a way of pretending to lower your status in front of the other person. Whoever bows lowest wins!

In the West we also use similar rituals as with gifts and seating arrangements in formal settings. Who sits at the captain's table? Who eats in the kitchen?

It used to be the case that families would gather together at mealtimes. Breaking bread together has been a tradition forever, it seems, although nowadays, it can be quite rare for all the members of one family to eat together, other than at times such as Thanksgiving or religious festivals. Some religious orders impose a Rule of Silence at mealtimes, and if you've ever partaken of a meal under such circumstances, you may have found it incredibly frustrating. Surely this is the time to talk to each other?

Where do deals get done? Over lunch! You need time to both enjoy the company as well as enjoy the meal. Think of the importance, socially, of breaking bread together. Eating is sharing, not just food, but of yourself, your hospitality. It's the traditional way of welcoming strangers.

My son, Max, was used to eating meals at the table with family while growing up. That all changed when he went off to college. He, like many of his friends, ate in the dining hall when possible, but mostly ate on the run, between classes. As school work got more complicated, eating meals with friends was the occasional pizza while studying. At work, Max would feel the need to get out and share a meal at lunch in order to solidify work relationships and get back to the feeling of breaking bread with family.

Whatever happened to the lunch hour?

Suzannah Hills (2013) has pointed out how breaks have been reduced to just 29 minutes because we're too busy:

- "Just one in five employees takes the traditional hour-long lunch break
- Majority of workers take less than half an hour for lunch
- Sacrificed break time adds up to 128 hours per year – 16 extra full work days
- One in seven said they hoped to impress their boss by taking shorter breaks."

An OfficeTeam report provides a comment on US eating habits. (OfficeTeam, 2014)

Workers were asked, "What is the average length of your typical lunch break?" Their responses:

Less than 10 minutes/no break	9%
10-15 minutes	5%
16-20 minutes	2%
21-30 minutes	32%
31-45 minutes	11%
60 minutes or more	38%
Don't know/no answer	4%

Cultural Differences

I discovered a restaurant in Chicago that had no seats. You had to eat standing up. Great food, but people were in and out in about five to ten minutes. It was like eating on the run. Compare this to the French lunchtime, which can last up to two hours, and usually involves a lot of chatting. Once, when I was eating lunch at an international conference, I noticed the stunning cultural differences. For example, I noticed that other Americans (including myself) had death grips on their silverware and spoke often with food-filled mouths. The French, however, put down their silverware to talk and took their time. Others used their utensils like conductor's batons waving wildly for emphasis. When watching the French, I just thought, "Pick up that fork and start shoveling, we've got presentations to attend."

Other cultures share much more time in eating together. Every festive occasion in France involves some kind of communal meal – often eaten at long lines of trestle tables out of doors, even along the street – a regular kind of street party. Any kind of get-together would usually end with a meal or a glass of something. I used to think that the main reason for any activity was the shared food and drink, that the work you had done before that was of secondary importance.

Think about your own community and its attitude toward shared meals. Over our lifetimes, the style of mealtimes has varied considerably. At one time, every meal was a sit-down at the table. Then came the television as the focus in the room. This isolated family members, as they were no longer facing each other. This way of doing things then gradually morphed into even more individuality, where members of the family would hardly ever eat together, preferring to graze or snack or otherwise fend for themselves regardless of what anyone else was doing.

If you are an eating-alone kind of person on an everyday basis, consider getting all the family together more often to have a shared meal. In the old days, this was traditional for Sunday lunch, although that often became a ritual with undesirable side-effects, because it was seen as obligatory to invite certain relatives, regardless of how well they fitted into the family group. At such mealtimes members of the family didn't always see eye-to-eye, or behaved outrageously (because this was happening in private behind closed doors) or too structured. These kinds of issues could easily be avoided in our more egalitarian society if each participant were to take some responsibility for making it work – either by preparing food – an enjoyable activity when done collaboratively – or organizing the context in which the shared meal is to take place.

Breaking bread with strangers

After the 2015 earthquakes in Nepal, it was reported that helpers who arrived in devastated villages – the houses had collapsed, there was complete chaos and lack of facilities – were offered food by the now homeless inhabitants. That had always been their custom: you welcomed strangers by offering food. Now, even in this time of food shortage, the tradition was still strong.

One winter in France, when out for a walk, we met a lone traveler. At the time we were living on the route of le Chemin / el Camino de Compostela – the ancient pilgrim route to Santiago in Spain. Throughout the year, pilgrims passed through the village, making this long journey by foot. Most of them came in the summer, but one day at the end of January we met a Swiss woman who was making the journey alone. We were surprised, but recognizing that she would be alone in the hostel, just along the road, we invited her to join us in a simple meal that evening. She readily accepted. She was on a personal journey; she and her husband had reached a crisis point, and she had decided that one way to sort herself out was to walk the pilgrimage route, of over 1000 miles, to gain clarity on her situation. We met her at roughly the half-way point. After she left us, she crossed the Pyrenees in some of the coldest weather of the year. However, she did promise to send us a postcard when she got to Santiago. It was some months later the card arrived. She had achieved her goal, and more. Her husband had driven from Switzerland in order to collect her at the end of her journey; whatever had happened between them had been resolved.

This story has a number of metaphorical meanings. The journey made by oneself, in which one finds oneself. It's not essential to walk a thousand miles, but it is often useful to take yourself out of a situation which needs clarity, so that you get time alone. This has an effect on the other person who has been left behind – time to think.

In fact, quite a number of pilgrims use such a journey to gain a new perspective on life. We admire their determination, their aim, and appreciate the simple meeting of fellow-travelers on the path of life.

CHAPTER 14
Being Realistic About the Difficulties of Change

I F WISHES WERE HORSES ...
You want to have better relationships. So is setting positive goals the answer? It is certainly a good idea to get clear about what you want for yourself, for and from other people, as well as your work and where you want to be in so many years time. But positive thinking – despite its extensive promotion over recent decades – is simply not enough by itself. Just thinking positively can be counterproductive because it stops you thinking things through thoroughly.

So think of what you want. And then imagine that you've got it. Great. Now, what happens next? How is your life different? What have you yet to learn?

The psychologist Gabriele Oettingen (Oettingen, 2014) and her colleagues ran a series of experiments designed to assess how effective having positive fantasies about the future was. She discovered that spending time and energy thinking about how well things could go actually reduces most people's motivation to achieve them. Because you have visualized the end result, you've fooled your brain into thinking you've already got it, so it stops bothering about it. It's still a good idea to think carefully about what you want, and to make your desired outcomes SMART, or whatever, but more is required if you are going to increase the probability of achieving your desires. Oettingen suggests that a better strategy is to think ahead about all the possible challenges and downsides of going for that particular outcome, so that you still have something extra to work for. You know from experience that there are always trials and setbacks – those unforeseen events that make life interesting.

These extras include considering the worst-case scenario: what could possibly go wrong? Yeah, you have to face up to the fact that life doesn't always turn out the way you want it. Think through some contingency plans: if something awful did happen, what would you do? Are you prepared for this? Do you have a Plan B … or Plan C? A fall-back position? It's a good idea to set a cut-off point beforehand so that if things do diverge from plan, you know when to cut your losses rather than throw more money at a project that is never going to deliver. This applies to relationship-seeking as well. At what point should you stop pursuing it and direct your attentions elsewhere? When you reach that point, be realistic. It's never going to work. Time to rethink. It's rather like bidding in an auction – you set your maximum ahead of time: this far and no further. The idea is that in the heat of the moment, when the juices are running, you have a small sensible voice telling you it's time to quit. The heart will want to override that decision, so be firm.

Apart from those plan-scuppering contingencies, how will you make sure that things stay on track? That may take more time and effort than you imagined. Few projects run to schedule; there are often unexpected events that change the need for the particular goal or the means of reaching it. For example, someone else has just invented a system that makes your idea redundant, or made a technological advance which means your project can now move ahead faster. Laws change, political systems get revised, world events happen, so you'll need to adapt, and demonstrate enough flexibility to adjust your plans on the fly. In relationship terms, the person you have your eye on meets someone else and gets caught up in a hormonal surge that leaves you on the sidelines. Or the friend you've just made announces they have been offered a better job in a distant city, so Adios. Even the inevitable event of your children leaving the nest to go to college, predictable as it is, has to be faced with a degree of rational thought: how are you going to adjust your life now that they have gone?

So it's time to do some analytical thinking here, for the good and the not-so-good. If you try to cut out the process and effort parts, and skip ahead to visualizing yourself in some future reality with the perfect partner, the money, the yacht, the fast car and so on, then you are living in the land of dreams. If you'd imagined a life with that other person, but now they're gone, where's your strategy for moving forward? Are you really going to devote all your time to those activities and sports that you've put on hold over the years? Really? There's nothing wrong with dreams, but lower your expectations and bring them down to earth, because that way you are more likely to have a future you'll enjoy.

I've said it before, but it's worth saying again. Forget the dream of telling yourself that you're going to live happily ever after. You're focusing on the wrong thing: how you think you'll feel. The trouble with this is that if you are deliberately trying to make yourself feel happy and you keep checking your Happy-meter, then your lack of progress, your lack of perfection, is often the very thing that makes you feel miserable. So stop paying so much attention to your inner self, and switch your focus onto doing worthwhile things for and with other people.

CHAPTER 15
I'll Start Procrastinating Tomorrow ...

OVERCOMING INERTIA
"Have I really got to do this?" "Where's my willpower gone?" You reach a threshold where you flip from not wanting to do something to action stations. You'd think by now that you would find it easy to put yourself in motion, because you're making changes, getting things done all the time. In the world of self-help books, making changes is often promoted as something easy. But in many cases overcoming resistance and inertia are challenging problems. It's a bit like the problem with positive thinking – you imagine doing something, and your brain then powers down because it thinks you've already done it. That's a great way to give in to procrastination. Plus there's our inherent ability to provide stories that explain what's going on. This is especially true with stuff around relationships. "He got out of the wrong side of the bed this morning." "Perhaps she's just having a bad day. It will pass." "I know they don't really mean that." And we give them the benefit of the doubt. Perhaps you misread the situation and now find yourself accused of over-reacting, making a mountain out of a molehill. So you put it off … once more. Do you really have to wait until it blows up in your face? You know what that's like! In the doghouse for days after.

Taking positive action means bypassing all that stuff, all the thinking about it, weighing the pros and cons, which will usually end up with finding reasons for not doing something and pretending that it will blow over. Put aside your habitual way of doing things for a moment (rest assured, they'll still be there for you later). Turn off those internal voices you hear, from the part of your mind that looks after you and wants to make you safe. That's what you're up against – the strong desire to protect, because that often means not changing but rather maintaining the status quo.

In everyday practical terms, a useful tip is that if you can do something in less than five minutes, then just do it. No excuses. You may protest, "I'm just waiting for the right moment", but that never comes. With relationship issues, you have no way of knowing whether now is a good time to sort something out quickly, or whether it's a biggie. Once you start, you find that it could take hours, days or rumble on for weeks or longer. That's why later in the book, I suggest that you can take swift action by making an appointment to discuss things later (Chapter 34). However, if you think that it can be dealt with quickly, then take action now. *Just do it.* You may have come across this piece of advice before. You may have it in cross-stitch and framed on the wall. Doesn't mean it doesn't apply to you. You could easily have blown up the confrontation into a full-length movie – with a sequel – and you could be entirely wrong. You won't know until you stop thinking about it and imagining all kinds of catastrophes and actually confront the other person. Not provocatively, but enquiringly, "There's something I need to say. Is this a good time?" Then say your piece. The response may just be "OK" or possibly, "I need to think about that. Let's get together later and discuss it." Whatever happens, you will know what to do. And you'll be pleased you took action now.

Not convinced? You have done this before. Remember a time when you did overcome your hesitations and came out with it. People are far more resilient than you might think. You don't see yourself as fragile or likely to crumble into a thousand pieces. If you can survive the slings and arrows, assume others can too (but watch the body language). Your intervention will adjust the relationship to some extent, so monitor what happens, and be flexible so that things turn out in a way that benefits you both.

Making use of feedback

This is a two-way thing. Other people are going to want to adjust you – and they will call it 'giving you feedback'. Formal feedback-giving has had a bad press – the annual review (information received far too long after the event), the feedback sandwich (you don't quite believe the sincerity of the praise; you're waiting for the "but ..."), or some harsh words spoken from a position of anger or resentment which becomes some kind of put-down. Probably not useful.

Feedback works better when you ask for it. "How can I improve my golf swing?" "How can improve my presentation so that people will be spurred into action?" With this kind of mindset, you are open to receiving helpful suggestions. However, these are often hard to come by. You need to ask someone who has been in your position and has learned the hard way how to improve (and who has convincing evidence to show their competence).

Some kinds of feedback can be helpful, especially when delivered fresh. One of the most effective ways of learning is to find out what you could improve, and then try it out right away (Lemov et al., 2012:114). This is the basis of making feedback effective. Feedback is just information for you about how you could do things differently. You get this by noticing the consequences of your actions, and also by other people telling you what you probably haven't noticed and that you could do better. This is where having friends you can trust is essential, because then you know they're being straight, not trying to belittle you.

Be proactive, ask them: "Can you tell me one thing I could do to improve?" One is quite enough; it gives you a specific focus. To maximize the benefit, make the change straight away. Don't think about it, discuss it, analyze it, or look it up on the internet – those are all delaying tactics and pretty much a waste of time. Just try it the new way, whatever it was, however embarrassing that might feel. It makes sense to do this while your coach/observer is still around so that you can then make finer adjustments. It also might feel embarrassing to demonstrate your under-par performance in front of an expert. But this is how we learn, so get over it. Do it, and both of you will notice the improvement and you'll be able to continue towards mastery.

Practice this in a safe context – not where your integrity, reputation or credibility is going to be put on the line. Start with small changes. One at a time. Dip your toe in to see what it's like.

And if someone asks you for feedback … Be kind. Think in terms of behavior, not in terms of character traits that they can't change. For example, "When you shake hands like that, I find that quite uncomfortable. Perhaps you could reduce the pressure of your grip?" If there is a list of things that you perceive the other person is doing wrongly then select the one item that is key, the one thing that if they changed it would cause many other things to readjust naturally. If you're not sure what that would be, ask them, "What do you think would make the most difference to what you're wanting to do?" because it's quite likely they do have some idea, and need some external confirmation.

So put this into practice right away. What's the one thing you could do that would get you to do things straight away, rather than putting them off?

CHAPTER 16
Communication

Much unhappiness has come into the world because of
bewilderment and things left unsaid.
~ DOSTOYEVSKY

ONE THING MOBILE PHONES DO for you is they enable you to
talk to other people in situations which previously would
have been impossible. You encounter a solitary person
walking down the street, and as you pass by you catch a phrase
or two of their conversation with an invisible partner. They
ignore their visible passerby, hoping they won't intrude upon
your space (but fail). So what has happened in the world that we
have so much more to say to each other these days? Has talking
become a ritualized way of keeping in touch where the actual
content is minimal and probably not important? Monitor your
own conversations for a while if you want to answer that one.

The thing is that whenever you are in the presence of another
person, or talking to them on your phone, or via computer,
whether you are saying anything or not, whatever you are doing
or not doing, you are communicating with them to some degree.
People draw some conclusion from your very presence and . No
words need to be spoken. Simply being there says something
about you because they will be reading you, noticing your body
language and assessing your status.

It's easy to be misunderstood. Much of what passes for
communication is a fill-in-the-blanks guessing game. Words
given the illusion of being precise, definitive, but the reality
is somewhat different. Language always has a degree of
vagueness, although most of the time we manage to get along,

because we have a shared experience of the meaning of the words used. But there's more to it than the actual words used; language is complex. Does someone call a spade a spade or do they beat about the bush? Do they tell it like it is, or beat around the bush? Some people often like to be told things straight – no faffing around, no euphemisms. For example, would you like to be told "We're letting you go"? How would you respond? "What, you mean I'm living in a prison?"

Tone of voice is important; others interpret your attitude from the tone of voice you're using. Sometimes the associated emotion is what's being communicated, and the actual words are irrelevant. Can you tell if someone is joking, being deliberately rude or merely ironic? Can you switch into a creative mode of communicating, telling stories, imagining a hypothetical future, musing about probabilities: "What if ...?" "I'm wondering ...?" "Have you ever thought about ...?" Most of us are adept at switching our way of communicating to suit our need.

This part of the book covers some key aspects of communication. Another huge subject; it's impossible to cover it all. So here are some practical things about language and communication, with some tips on how to increase the probability of getting other people to do what you want – which, after all, is the basic assumption of all acts of communication.

Intention

When you open your mouth, you do it for a reason: you want to inform or affect the other person in some way. You may want to tell them about a funny incident, or what you want to say is important and you want a strong reaction from them. Shouting "Fire!" demands a response, as does, "I want you to take out the garbage, now." How do you want your audience to respond when you tell them that boring old story about your vacation?

It's not always clear what the underlying intention is. It could be deliberately hidden (we all have our diplomatic and hidden agendas) or we may not be sure of it ourselves and are stumbling around trying to find the words to express our half-formed ideas.

Intentions can be inconsequential: "Nice weather." We're engaging in social lubrication, keeping relationships going, staying on good terms: "How are you doing in your new job?" Or quite specific: "Can you always copy me in on your emails to Company X?"

Some talk is just to inform the other person that we're there ("Hi") or to give an updated report on how we are – the face-to-face equivalent of our blogs, tweets, selfies and so on. You give others the benefit of your observations on your life, what you are currently paying attention to, or given the opportunity, you recount your personal history, the story of your life. Or you may just want to express your thoughts, ideas, opinions, judgments, theories, decisions: how you would like the world to be, how you want things to be different in the future, and how you intend to achieve these things.

Your intention may be to somehow improve the lives of others. This is why we inform, teach, instruct, or otherwise intervene in other people's lives. "It's for their benefit" goes the rationale. Part of this two-way communication involves you responding to other people – listening, answering their questions, clarifying points, or generally making things clear, because all language is ambiguous at times.

So let's look at different kinds of communication and how they work. Here is a list of some of the reasons why we choose to communicate with each other. Essentially, nearly every piece of communication is about wanting someone else to do something that they are not yet doing.

Expressing our intentions

- *Clarification* – To define, explain. "Oxytocin is a hormone which affects sociability and feeling good."
- *Observations* – To give information. What you're paying attention to at the moment: "The wind is strong today." To clarify, specify, make clear or provide facts – "It's Harvey here", "I used to live in New York."
- *Thoughts, ideas* – Your way of making sense of the world, your opinions, judgments, theories, decisions.
- *Feelings* – To draw attention to your emotional state, how you feel, how you are reacting to what's going on. How I feel in myself; how I feel about you. You may even be trying to suppress this information by closing down – which the other person might see as being resistant, unwilling to reveal information or to comply with their wishes.
- *Needs* – What I want for myself.
- *Wants* – What I want you to do.
- *Changes* – How you want to change the other person, or their perception of the world in some way, so that they act differently, or understand things differently. You may be giving instructions or teaching them to do something.
- *Status* – Assert your relative status to emphasize your status, maintain your position in the hierarchy
- *Creativity* – To play, have fun, to muse, create something new.

Are you sure about that?

We've all become smarter through the spread of technology, with formidable googling skills. If you give people facts, it's now very easy to check their validity. Some people will do this right in front of you, just because they can. You can be challenged on everything coming out of your mouth by someone with a smartphone. At our fingertips, we have access to a significant amount of information about our world. This makes it more difficult to come across as an expert in anything.

A travel friend of mine keeps a smartphone in his hand at all times. This person is one of the smartest people I know. He's a physician with degrees from Harvard, Stanford, and Johns-Hopkins. Yet he has a thirst for continuous knowledge. We were on a trip to Cabo San Lucas a few years ago. We went to go whale watching and saw this huge personal yacht at the dock while we waited for our dinghy. Before I knew it, Dr. Bob had information about the size, capacity, and owner of the yacht. My daughter-in-law also has her smartphone with her. The problem with that is that now I can't make stuff up as frequently as I used to – it keeps me honest. When I mention some statistic that I read somewhere, she immediately verifies it on her phone. I hate having to be accurate. But, then again, Albert Einstein, when asked for his definition of intelligence, said that intelligence is not the ability to store information, it's the ability to know where to go to find information. He even had to go to the phone book to look up his own phone number.

How's that again?

"Honey, have you seen my whatchamacallit?"
"When did you last see it?"
"You know, when I was using it the other day."
"It's probably with all the others."

Although you might think that language can be quite precise (it can be in some specialized contexts, think: ordering sushi or parts for your car), on the whole it is rather imprecise, and open to misinterpretation. Actually, that's only from your point of view. You think you're being precise, but the person you're talking to thinks you're being rather vague and could do better. Communication is a process of refinement which comes from learning how each person uses language in different contexts according to their emotional state and what they want. Over time, as your relationship with the other person develops, you get better at understanding each other's intentions and their verbal idiosyncrasies. You may or may not know what 'my whatchamacallit' is. It depends on the context, what was happening the other day. An outsider wouldn't stand a chance. You are in the privileged position of having half a chance of knowing what it's about. You have acquired a version of the language that makes sense to you – on a good day – but will be unintelligible to outsiders, who supposedly speak the same language.

The problem is the common use of pronouns to describe what are actually nouns. Wouldn't it have been better to say, "Where'd you put the plunger, dear?" Now, wouldn't it? One of the greatest barriers to a successful relationship is the laziness of assumptions. We assume that just because we know what we're thinking, the other person should automatically be able to read our minds and respond with clarity of understanding. And then we get mad at the other person for not listening to us. Just how stupid is that?!

Maybe other people do that to you; they expect you to know things without being told. They treat you as though you are a mind-reader who can divine their needs and desires. Alas, this is not true, though from long experience you may get surprisingly good at picking up on minimal cues about what they want. If you really must know what the whatchamacallit is, then the tedious way is to backtrack through what they've said and clarify every vague word. It annoys them, thinking "Isn't it obvious?", and it frustrates you, "I ought to know this."

Professional and technical people establish an in-group language that sets them apart. Any newcomers to the profession need to pick this up rapidly if they are to get on. Same with people and their hobbies and leisure interests. They develop a specialized vocabulary with its jargon, abbreviations, and shortcuts to meaning that go with the words Trouble starts when they tend to spout this stuff to anyone they are talking to, whether a member of that group or not. To the uninitiated, they are just plain unintelligible. When I first went to work for the government, I was given a lexicon – a book of abbreviations of longer terms. It was 503 pages long. The idea was you could save time, space, and breath by using these shortcuts to describe everything from ideas, products, processes, people. For example, we'd talk glibly about CAROB (The Center for Applied Research on Organizational Behavior). The problem was that almost every person had to stop and look up the meaning in the lexicon – which actually took up more time. I can picture the person sitting in the windowless room downstairs writing out more shortcuts and snickering to themselves "That's a good one."

Such lexicons separate people into tribes. Those who know what the abbreviations and acronyms mean and those who don't. The insiders and the outsiders; those who can feel special and those who don't belong.

CHAPTER 17
Transaction Costs & Communication Preferences

AS IN MANY OTHER AREAS of life, we have our individual preferences for how we like information to be given to us, how we tend to organize words ourselves. The question arises: do you adapt to the other person or not? If you don't have the time or the flexibility to get to know everyone's foibles, then you may just need to educate everyone about "This is the way we're going to do things."

Every communication requires time and effort. It's possible to reduce these by establishing 'the way we communicate in certain situations' using code-words, gestures, hand signals, or whatever. Could even be the raising of an eyebrow. Not every shortcut works, though. The UK government set up a health advisory and guidance organization that they originally called NICE – catchy title, but because this was too common a word, each time it was mentioned the newsreader would give it in full: the National Institute of Clinical Excellence – so no time saved there!

There was a fad some years ago for differentiating language into visual, auditory and kinesthetic styles of learning. This arose out of the observation that some people see what you mean, for others it sounds good, while others feel that you're creating a stink ... The idea was that people, especially children, had a preferred way of learning, and that if you adapted your teaching to these styles the children would learn more effectively. The onus was on the teacher to adapt, to be flexible – no bad thing. Alas, research showed that such learning styles were not supported by any evidence. When you think about it, the traditional system is far more useful in that it promotes flexibility in the learner which is essential, given that they are going to encounter a range of presentational styles during their lifetime.

If you are with one individual, then it may save a lot of time and effort to demonstrate your flexibility and match their preferred way. But that's not going to work with a group. So be yourself, and make sure you make yourself clear and cover most of the bases. So for example, start with why you are telling them something, because that will grab their interest, rather than giving you the "Why are you telling me this?" puzzled look. Give the big picture, and then the details. You know this stuff – you've been exposed to stories and Hollywood movies all your life. It's just that you got involved so much with the content that you had no spare capacity to notice the structure – *how* the story was being told.

Psychological Context

We also have preferred ways of dealing with the information we are getting. Although we think it's clever to do lots of things at the same time – multi-tasking – the evidence is that we're not actually that good at it, and in a work situation, spreading our attention to several different tasks actually makes our performance worse on each of them. That's because we have to keep switching from one to the other, and our mental start-up routine kicks in each time.

We keep coming back to this idea of limited conscious mental capacity. It's something we can't actually do much about. This is where the brain-as-computer analogy breaks down: we can't just slot in some more RAM. Limited mental workspace is a reality; we will make life easy for ourselves by not overdoing things. Not a cop-out, just being realistic. It will reduce stress. Single-tasking is the way to go.

What travels through our ears shares the same neural pathway as short-term memory. This can prove hazardous at times. Often when we hear something, we become temporarily deaf to information that sounds similar … so we think we heard something that actually wasn't said. Or don't hear something that was actually said. This can be dangerous in situations where not hearing important information or critical instructions could lead to disaster (even death). Interpretation is also dependent upon the specific context, so make sure you're attuned to that. If you're the one initiating, then put your audience in the picture first: "Today I'm going to be talking about communication styles" or "I'd like to ask you about the work you do."

When we are busy concentrating, it's often the case that we power down our hearing, and then miss what someone else is saying to us. That happens when we're busy inside our own mind, dreaming of other things – until a sudden noise brings us back to the present, the noise being your name or a remark along the lines of "You never listen to what I'm saying!" And that's how many arguments begin, because you listen for a while and then switch off incoming information briefly while you process what you have just heard. So if you are the one delivering, allow your listeners time to reflect on the content. Obviously you think it's important, so they will need time to digest. So give your attention to them rather than running on; watch and wait to know when it's OK to continue.

Sequential – Random

We also have preferences for how we like to get and sort information. The default setting is sequential: one thing after another. Gradually the picture builds up. But this isn't to everyone's liking. Some are happy with information coming in randomly, in no particular sequence, as with the clues in a crime drama. Maybe that's how you like to study. You wander around, getting bits from here and there, and then go through some kind of digestion process, and blend everything into a pattern. However, there is always the problem of bias creeping in, because what we get first influences how we sort what comes later.

There are also opportunities for mismatching other people here. Have you ever had that experience of wanting what you've just heard repeated or clarified? You ask the other person to say the last bit again, because you didn't quite catch it or it wasn't quite clear, "Could you tell me that bit again?" and they go right back to the beginning and you get their whole spiel again, repeated more or less word for word. "No, just the last bit I didn't get." That's a shift they find hard to make. For them, the linear format is how it's stored in their mind, and they do not understand how it could be any different. One strategy would be to briefly summarize their story, fast-forwarding from the beginning up to the point where you want more detail. For example, "OK, so you've told me how you got into this, and the training course you went on, and now you're working with the team on Project X. So tell me, how exactly is your team organized? How did you allocate the roles?"

Big Picture – Nitty-gritty Details

Another kind of difference is the scale of the information people prefer to work with. Some prefer the broad sweep of life, to talk about their visions for the future, for the masses. These people reputedly become the leaders and CEOs of organizations, because of their ability to think in generalities, the big picture. This greater scope allows for strategic thinking. It often includes connections to what else is going on in the world. The downside of that is that you lose the details. Someone who prefers thinking big has a vision of what's possible. A vision is about expanding, diversifying, moving forward – you get the picture – and you leave the practical details to others – that's their job. So you get instructions of a general nature: "Go and find out" or "Get this done properly" which gives you little to work with if you need guidance on how to complete the task correctly.

On the other hand, others really like the nitty-gritty details. This is fine if you're programming or doing research. Not so good if you're moving up the management hierarchy and find it hard to let go. So you end up engaged in micro-managing, spelling out every little detail, not really trusting anyone else to do what took you years to learn.

How do you get on with these different kinds of people? You need to be flexible so that you can realize where they are coming from and adapt what you say to the same level. There's no point asking the visionary, "Well, what size screws are we going to use?" That just breaks the spell, and causes them bewilderment that you asked such a stupid question. How would they know? Well, they may actually know the answer, but that's not the purpose of the interaction. With nitty-gritty people, it's a good idea to ask them to think in broader terms once in a while: "Think about why you're assembling this device, how it fits into the company's business." "Remember that people are coming to see us to have a good time – not to evaluate our choice of silverware."

CHAPTER 18
Establishing and Maintaining Relationships

"GOOD TO MEET YOU"
It's become a bit of a cliché to be reminded that you never get a second chance to make a first impression. Given that the other person has summed you up in a fraction of a second, often from across the room before you got in close-communication range, then trying to make adjustments to your habitual way of being yourself is going to be futile. What you can do is to be present and alive in this relationship with this person right now.

First of all, come out of your protective shell – that's where you're focused inside, probably engaging in an internal dialog with yourself, providing a running commentary on the world and how you fit into it – and make contact with this other person. Forget about yourself – they're the one that matters. Instead of defending your position, be open enough to go along with where they want to take you. Listen. Above all, don't block them. Blocking is a defensive habit that most of us engage in. The other person makes a suggestion, and we immediately go into negative mode and the conversation comes to halt. "What's your favorite TV program?" "Oh, I don't watch TV." Or "Shall we go to the cinema?" "No, I'm washing my hair tonight." Recognize when you are doing this, and decide to not do it when there is no real reason why you shouldn't. The consequence of continual blocking is that people won't bother to say anything to you because it's no fun for them.

Phatic communication – the verbal hand-shake

This is the technical term given to the grunts and pleasantries we make which essentially announce our presence or make a greeting. It's our way of keeping in touch with each other, how we maintain good relationships by being friendly, sociable, polite, formal.

Phatic communication is for setting the scene. It's not meant to do anything else; it's not deep discussion. So we choose safe subjects – the weather is very popular. What is important about talking this way is that we are actually talking to each other, acknowledging each other's presence, and keeping the wheels of human interaction turning.

It is conventional to greet other people, according to how well you know them, with terms ranging from "How do you do?" to "Hi." The noises we make are ritualistic, not to be taken at face value. For example, being asked "How are you?" does not require providing a full medical report. All you say is "Fine. And you?" and this does not have anything to do with how fine you're feeling at the time. The other person will pick up more of how you are feeling anyway, and will usually be too polite to comment.

However, not everyone, at all times, is willing or ready to disclose personal details. So you get the answer "I'm fine." What a wonderful blocking response that is! It doesn't mean what it says, it just says "I don't want to talk about this." From the context, and the history of your relationship – unless you have a deep personal connection to them, it's not a good idea to respond with "No, you're not!" You have to decide whether to let them be, or whether to probe – they may actually want you to do this. It's like they're checking whether *you* are the right person to explore this with.

How're you doing?

Once you have got through the preliminaries, you get to the meat in the communication sandwich (the bread being the opening and closing ritualistic remarks).

Wherever you are, you're always in a particular place, and that context brings with it expectations of how to behave, and what kind of communication is appropriate and likely to occur. In a formal or neutral environment such as a shop, a church, a synagogue, or in a restaurant you would expect certain typical kinds of behavior. The people there do their job and you don't expect to discover too much about their current emotional state or their problems at home. However, there's been something of a trend over recent years – something to do with customer care training in the service industry – and now the people who do things for you are more friendly, sometimes genuinely want to please you, rather than resembling the automatons of yesteryear. This is more than the programmed "Have a nice day"; people are more open and actually enjoy helping you. You have to decide how much to give back in return. In general, we tend to match other people in the level of personal disclosure. Again, it's a matter of judgment. I'm sure that if you start to tell the waiter or ticket clerk the whole of your life history, they will find an excuse to leave.

With friends and close associates it's different. You already know something about these people – their family, their home life – because that's part of sharing their lives with you. So when they are obviously not in a good state, they may wish you to respond without having to tell you. They expect you to ask. This is not the ritual "How are you doing?" This is genuine concern. "I really want to know how you are."

Attitude

If you've ever been to a workshop or training on communications, you have probably been told that the message that is sent is mostly non-verbal – somewhere between 90 to 93 percent. Although this sounds impressive, and gets you to reconsider how you think about the way you communicate, it is in fact a well-established urban myth based on some very constrained work done by the psychologist Albert Mehrabian in the 1960s. This myth has been doing the rounds ever since. Although it has been discredited, including by Mehrabian himself, it's a zombie idea that just won't die. So what can we pick out of this that is valid? Well, communication is not just in the words we use. Even when you write an email or text you are transmitting something of yourself. You may want to make a joke, or be ironic, which is not easy with just text, so you add emoticons to indicated how it's meant to be taken. Yes, indeed, there are these different aspects of communication, but the percentages given are meaningless, because there are so many ways in which we can and do communicate.

Keeping in touch, by whatever means

If we want the full range of information about the other person, we need direct face-to-face communication. When we can't manage face-to-face, we get by using email, texting, or messages on Facebook, and so on. These devices give us variable amounts of information about how we're feeling. The next big thing could be an app designed by scientist Rana el Kaliouby (Kaliouby, 2015) which offers a new technology that reads the expression on your face and matches it to the corresponding emotion.

Voice tonality is available when you talk on the phone. Having pictures helps, as on Skype, for example, but still we're losing a lot of information. Using emoticons and smileys in our emails and texts … good try, but they don't really do it for us. But face-to-face allows us to really show our talent, to pick up on the subtleties, because there is always much more going on that we could pay attention to – even too much at times. We're in there, fully engaged in all senses (mostly out of conscious awareness) and fully in the process, deriving unseen benefits from our human contact (and we are in range for touching).

In a general sense, we pick up what we call 'attitude'. We learn to read between the lines – the way the person's feeling, their posture, from the tone of their voice. The problem is that the tone of your voice is often affected by forces outside of your control. As with your level of happiness, your tone of your voice will vary with your biochemistry. As a result, you could be sending out signals that are very different from what you intend. If, for example, you didn't get enough sleep the night before, your message may be interpreted as lack of interest; no, you are simply tired. Or you may be perceived as angry when you just might be hungry (also referred to as 'hangry').

To overcome this potential misinterpretation of your message, you need to tell the person you're talking to something about your current state of mind and the reason for your current attitude. (But be aware of saying "I'm fine" – see above.) For example, I might say to Bob (in a slow, dragged down tone of voice), "Bob, I need to see you in my office". Bob might think he did something wrong. But if instead I say, "Bob, I was up all night last night taking care of my sick puppy and didn't get enough sleep … and I'm really tired", Bob might not be so freaked out by the tone of your voice because you explained it away; it becomes easier for Bob to understand the message you are sending the way it was intended. If by contrast, I were to say "Hey, Bob, got a moment? Somethin' to tell ya!" in a bright, breezy, excited voice, and I welcome Bob in with open arms into my office, then Bob's going to think he's on to something great.

Ambiguity

A guy walks into a bar, orders a drink, slams it down, throws $10 on the bar and runs out. Got the picture? The bartender slowly picks up the money, slowly turns to a   patron sitting at the

bar and says, "Huh, that guy was in such a hurry
that he forgot to pay for his drink ... but he left
me a $10 tip."

If you don't tell someone else how you want them to interpret
your information, they are going to act in their own self-interest.
And I can guarantee that their priorities are going to be different
than yours. You need to let others know what your intentions are
so they know how to react to your behavior.

You say: "It's clear to me what I mean." Well, yes, that's often
the case. But can you explain it to someone else? That's the
question to be asking. What seems obvious to you – because you
have all the information – may be not at all obvious so someone
else who is new to this idea. Assuming that others do have
your background is known as The Curse of Knowledge (Heath
Brothers, 2007). Take a moment to recall how you acquired your
understanding. It wasn't instant was it? It was probably a bit
tough at first, and you had to work at it. Now, though, it seems
easy, because you've made it your own. The curse is that there
is just no way of going back to your state of ignorance. Can't do
it. There's just no way of regressing to that not-knowing state of
innocence, and that makes it hard to empathize with the other
person. So, if it took you a while to grasp something, assume it
will be the same for others and cut them some slack. Or rather,
give them a helping hand.

Before you simply assume that other people understand you and
your behavior, do some checking out. What is their background
in all this, what do they already know? Check that they are
familiar with some of the key terms you use. For example, if
they haven't heard of the invisible gorilla effect (Chabris &
Simons 2011) then bring them up to speed on it. Just assuming
they are like you or that "It's obvious what to do", will land you
in trouble.

CHAPTER 19
Attraction – Chemistry 101

"The fact remains that getting people right is
not what living is all about anyway. It's getting
them wrong that is living, getting them wrong
and wrong and wrong and then, on careful
reconsideration, getting them wrong again. That's
how we know we're alive: we're wrong. Maybe
the best thing would be to forget being right or
wrong about people and just go along for the ride.
But if you can do that – well, lucky you."
~ *American Pastoral* by Philip Roth (1997)

WHAT ATTRACTS PEOPLE? 'Chemistry' is a rather vague term often used by Hollywood film critics when discussing whether the lead characters in a movie simulate a genuine relationship with each other. It probably comes down to: do they actually like each other and enjoy working together? This leaves us to wonder whether chemistry can be faked by actors. Given our understanding of reading people's faces, it seems that chemistry is hard to fake, and relatively easy to detect – rather in the way that a false smile is easy to spot. Once we study micro-expressions (Ekman, 2007) we understand that to a trained observer hiding our real feelings is not possible. So chemistry would appear to have validity. It indicates an actual liking, and any pretense is revealed by the camera lens.

OK, so what is the magic that draws people together? Not just anyone will do; there are millions who don't stand a chance. We are very, very choosy. Some are more choosy than others.

Think about what you find attractive about certain other people. Can you identify these qualities or characteristics that swing the balance in someone's favor?

People tend to choose others for long-term relationships who are roughly the same level of attractiveness as they are. Research on physical attraction suggests that the most significant factors in what makes people look beautiful are the proportions of the face: big eyes wide apart, bilateral symmetry ... There's probably not a lot you can do about changing these things.

Do other people find you attractive? Research has shown that your guess is no better than chance. You imagine that others are using similar criteria to your own, but you are mistaken. People are looking for very specific things, and although you have these qualities, you take them for granted "Doesn't everyone do that?" *You* don't realize how special they are. As they say, Beauty is in the eye of the beholder, and it's not easy giving yourself that point of view.

Lipstick and Pigs

"You remind me of someone I used to know…" We bring a lot of baggage to every new encounter that influences our perception of the other person, rose-tinted or otherwise. It's easy to transfer our knowledge of one person over to someone completely different, simply because they look similar. What someone looks like is a powerful cue for memories. We may then feel attracted to them simply because they exhibit one quality that we found appealing in a previous relationship. And then we pile on them all kinds of qualities, both good and bad, without justification. If the memory is positive, then we immediately start liking the person without going through the usual induction period. The other person may find this a bit strange. If, on the other hand, the memory is negative – they remind you of that bully at school, or that shifty bloke you met on vacation who tried to swindle you – then you have then cast an unjustified and damning slur on this person without them having anything to say about the matter.

This is the danger in stereotyping people. It's the perennial problem of wanting a short cut to knowing someone. Sure, it's a quick way to get a sense of who they are (and we do this all the time), but it's also very easy to be mistaken. Just because they have piercings or tattoos does not make them punks or whatever your current thought is. The trouble is, we're kind of doing this all the time, but we're not aware that we are doing it. It could account for the people you just do not get on with. It's also possible that you don't know why. Even when you think up reasons, the visual reminder is too strong, and that negative halo surrounds them. This is why you need to get up close and personal – to some degree – and find out more about them. Put your preconceived analysis on hold, ready to be surprised and delighted. And remember that truism that the more you get to know other people, the more of a mystery they become.

Where do our preferences spring from? We could imagine that they are from experiences very early in life, based on people who were around, or who we saw pictures of in magazines, on TV or in the movies. It's hard to know for sure. If you create a shopping list of the perfect partner you're likely to be attracted to someone who fulfills none of your criteria. Maybe the list motivates you to get out there and go looking, but then it becomes irrelevant.

We need to remind ourselves that we must manage with our limited understanding. Best thing is to enjoy the process of finding out more about the new person. The better you get to know them, the more the fantasy element decreases. With luck you discover how interesting they are in ways you had not dreamed of. Or disillusionment may come when you find just cause for thinking poorly of them, based on what they have to say or do that does not meet your standards. You could just as easily reject them based on what they believe, and how they subsequently behave: they treat people unfairly, or they're always looking for the negatives, they block your ideas and suggestions – they're glass-half-empty people. Or there is something about them that just doesn't lead to you feel that they are completely congruent. In that case, it's time to move on; you're not going to change them.

CHAPTER 20
Enhancing Relationships

HOW WAS YOUR DAY, DEAR? You're in a relationship where it's become common to talk about your day when you get back together in the evening or whenever. There are some tricky aspects of this: Who goes first? Who has had the most noteworthy day?

You know that your partner has been involved in an important event during the day. You might assume that they will be full of it, bursting to tell you the moment they walk in the door. So you stay quiet, waiting. But it doesn't come ... until a while later: "Well, aren't you going to ask me how it went?" You try to justify this: "I thought you'd want to tell me ..." Some people wait to be asked. So you'd better ask. It's a formality, it won't hurt you – unless you forget to do it. In my experience, saying "You don't need permission" or "If it's that important, you're going to tell me anyway" are not effective responses. So here's the low-status strategy again. Just ask "So how was your day? What happened?" Being humble is good, as long as you actually listen.

On the other hand, if you have had a momentous day, and you're bursting to tell, then perhaps you should consider if you really must go first. If that's your choice, then you may need a preliminary "Can I tell you about my day?" so that you get your partner's attention. Or at least that's the theory. Chances are they are also about to let loose with their own tale of woe or delight, and they're mentally rehearsing it as you speak. Which means they probably won't be able to give you their full attention until they've told their story. So could you wait, let them go first? Because you know your story will keep awhile. Here's an opportunity for setting the scene. Clear any worries out of the way, the urgent stuff. Get something to drink, go and sit comfortably, and then tell the tale.

It does sound terribly formal, this taking turns, asking polite questions. But it serves a purpose. It's as if you're serving hors d'oeuvres before the main course – you're getting a flavor of where the other person is at, their mental, emotional state. Are they ready for the big stuff, or do they need to recover after their busy day?

It's about not taking people for granted; your reading of their body-language may not be totally accurate. So check assumptions. Slow down for a moment and take soundings. Although some people expect you to know things without being told, it's better to assume you don't know, and then try to divine their needs and desires based on their body language and anything you may from long experience pick up using minimal cues. If you are still not sure, you'll need to gently ask "How are you? I want to know how you are." Touch may be appropriate here.

The problem with mind-reading

You're empathetic. You can easily put yourself is someone else's shoes, and walk several miles in them. You feel for them and you say, "I know exactly how you feel." Boom. Shut down. "No you don't!" What went wrong? You raised your status, you became the superior know-it-all, and this was not appreciated. What to do instead? You keep your status low – lower than theirs. The reality is that you do not know exactly how they feel – how could you – you're just guessing. So admit some level of uncertainty. Take the feeling you do have, your best guess, and push it out into the common space between you. "I guess you must be feeling pretty sore about what happened" or "That was quite a shock. I imagine you're probably angry at him for saying that?" Then you are more likely to get agreement, or a modification. "Yeah, I felt devastated, and a bit guilty" or "I was more than angry, I was furious!" What you are doing is using a conditional phrase to start: "I guess ...", "I imagine that ...", "I'm wondering if ..." in order to avoid the direct contradiction. Note that these days it's not advisable to use: "How do you feel about that?" as this question has become a source of mockery. It became over-used within the counseling world, and it now produces a sneer.

It's a fairly safe bet that there's always something else going on in that person's life which you do not know about. We all have our worries and concerns that we keep private. So when some incident occurs, the surface features may be a manifestation of an underlying issue. It's not a simple story; you don't have all the facts, and even if you did, it's complicated. Something is distracting them, and you have to decide how far you want to go in opening this particular can of worms. You could go for it: "So what is the big concern that you have going on right now?" or at least arrange a time later when you could discuss it (see Making an Appointment, Chapter 34).

Sometimes the dam bursts and your significant other pours out the burdens of their day onto you. Perhaps it's been a particularly stressful time and things were just not going in the expected direction. Without thinking, you started spouting off your brilliant suggestions for how you would handle the situation. You smile and commend yourself on how helpful you've just been. Then comes the surprise: the response you get is anger – directed at you. You wonder, "What did I do? I was just trying to be helpful." Well, you may have taken the wrong fork in the road. Switching the focus to yourself is not a good idea. "If I were in your situation I would be ... angry/confused/sad ..." Expressing how you would feel in similar circumstances diverts attention away from the person who needs your support, and you lose rapport.

How to avoid being dumped on

You will have no doubt met some people who wish to tell you all their problems, in great detail. People feel the need to vent, to talk about their day, or their medical condition – and all you're meant to do is listen, and agree with them. Asking questions for clarification only gets you in deeper. You, on the other hand, having plenty of your own issues, don't wish to know about their gallstones, or their irritable bowels. You need a way to halt the flow, so to speak.

They want to talk to you – or rather they want to talk *at* you, and you're in no mood to listen. Or you've heard it all before, and you know it's going nowhere. How long before you put a halt to it? It doesn't matter how long you stay neutral, bland, avoid offering any encouragement – they're not paying attention to you, just reveling in the sound of their own voice. Finally you crack: No More! You need to rebuff the other person – politely. You'll have to interrupt if you are going to get the message across that you are not going to take all their worries onboard.

The usual trick at a party or gathering is to suddenly spot "someone I have to talk to" over there and move away. You've seen this dozens of times in movies. But you can't do this so easily in a one-to-one situation, when you're buttonholed in the street, for example. If you see a potential encounter looming, then, because you know how this person operates, don't stop. The trick is not to slow down, but to give a hearty greeting "You all right?!", and keep moving: "Got to rush! See ya."

Should you get captured then the best strategy is to avoid giving them anything to latch onto. Don't ask questions, don't show interest. It's like you're presenting them with a featureless wall – imagine smooth ice – which they can't get a hold on. Should you respond with a minimum of interest, you've thrown them a lifeline, and in goes the piton: they've got you. Therefore, when you've heard enough and want to get away, the subtle way is to lean slightly towards them, place your hand lightly on their forearm, and say, in an intimate kind of way. "I'm sorry. I do have to go now." Straighten up, and say goodbye. If this isn't appropriate, you must be bolder: hold up your hands, palms towards them to indicate Stop. "I'm sorry, I'm very busy at the moment, and I just don't have time to listen. OK?" Leave. Don't hesitate. Don't look back.

I Don't Know

I don't know are three of the most important words you can invoke in any relationship. In the past, prior to the internet revolution, people were valued for their expertise ... the knowledge they had accumulated over years of experience and research. No one knew everything, so folks relied on the expertise of others. That mutual reliance on knowledge transfer created strong bonds between bosses/followers, coworkers, spouses, family members, friends, and so on. Knowledge accumulated gradually: hunched shoulders in dimly lit libraries, the ever stronger glasses for strained eyes in order to be worthy of a PhD. Now this can be supplanted by a smartphone with Ask.com. The value of the hard work of research has diminished. You can no longer extrapolate (make stuff up). As a result, it's clearer where the boundaries of knowledge lie, and educated people are more willing to use the phrase "I don't know" more often, and with more regret.

But fear not, it gets easier. Take a deep breath, look yourself in the eye in the mirror and repeat "I don't know" over and over again. Believe me, people will respect you more if you admit that for all your prior knowledge, you still don't know everything. Speculating gets you nowhere; it's the domain of journalists and political pundits – say no more. Saying "I don't know" puts people on the same footing. To find answers, everyone collectively goes into the research mode. When facts are discovered, everyone becomes an instant expert. By the way, the cachet of a PhD then changes from "one with the knowledge" to "one who knows how to analyze/think/translate facts into action" – oh, yeah, and to speculate.

As a result of doing masses of research reading, I've accumulated a myriad of small data points on wide ranging subjects. When an issue comes up, I tend to bring these bits together and devise a likely answer. My wife just says that I make shit up. The other day, she asked me a question and I started down my normal speculative road searching for an answer. Then it hit me. I really didn't know what the actual answer to the question she asked was. So I stopped, looked at her directly, and said, "I don't know." We both sat in silence for what seemed like an eternity. Then she said, "Thank you. That must have been hard." It was. Over the next few minutes we followed through with a low-tension discussion about the issue, where I for once wasn't acting like I actually knew the answer, because I didn't. Admitting ignorance opens up all sorts of possibilities for collaboration and positive interaction.

Saying "I don't know" lowers your status in a relationship which makes other person feel important, more powerful. People like to be consulted, like to demonstrate their expertise, just like you do. There will be many times when you don't know; the internet does not have all the answers, and not everything can be looked up. Some things you only find out by experiencing them directly. And that means recognizing the limits of your ever-expanding, but minuscule domain of knowledge. And that's humbling.

So what to do after you have acknowledged your ignorance? Start from the position that you are not alone here. Sure, there are domains of knowledge where no one knows the answer – and you'll find these areas have been sufficiently mapped out for you to feel justified in your ignorance. And when something goes wrong, or you don't know how to do something that you think you ought to know, then it's a safe bet to realize that someone else has already solved this problem. This is where the internet shines, and where you don't have to fumble around in the dark. Some of their illuminations may be a tad technical (computer nerds win hands down on this). So before you go searching for drivers to download or entering arcane codes into your registry because an external device fails to load and produces error messages, try the simple, traditional option: switch it off, unplug it, wait a few seconds and then plug it in again. These age-old remedies are sometimes the best.

Can you apply this same strategy to relationship issues? For certain, someone has had the problem before, and they may have resolved it effectively, but they may not have written it down, nor were they absolutely sure about what it was they did that worked. If you go searching for answers, remember to take them with a pinch of salt.

Applying solutions without first finding out more directly from your partner is not a good idea. Ask, "What have you already tried?" Or start by asking their opinion on what they want. You could even get them to speculate on the one thing that would make a difference, something they could change. Ask, "So what do you think might work?" Who knows, they may already have the solution without realizing it.

CHAPTER 21

Fear of Rejection

"Having not said anything the first time, it was
somehow even more difficult to broach the
subject the second time around."
~ DOUGLAS ADAMS

YOU OFFER A SUGGESTION … or rather, you think about
making the offer, but you hold back because you are not
sure how the other person will respond, and as they're
in a glass-half-empty mood, you think they will reject your
proposal.

Let's face it: many of your offers, suggestions, ideas, will
be rejected. Sometimes on a rational basis: too costly, too
complicated, too difficult, takes too long. And sometimes
emotional: the other person is not in the mood, or they don't
like you. Whatever. You'll never really know why people say
No to you. But get used to it. The way to do this is to make lots
of offers, knowing that most of them will be rejected. And then
you'll be happy when one of your suggestions is accepted and
acted upon.

It's about giving people choices. If you only give one possibility,
a 'take it or leave it' situation, then if they leave it, you've
nowhere to go. So give a choice of two: the red one or the
blue one? You are assuming that one of the options will be
chosen. Wise parents have been using this technique for years.
"Do you want me to read you a story before or after you clean
your teeth?" – which presupposes the cleaning of the teeth. It
works for grown-ups too. "Would you rather go to Florida or to
Europe?" presupposes a vacation somewhere. Of course, you'll

sometimes get the reply "Neither" but as you've been expecting some rejection this is not such a big deal. You backtrack: "Do you want a vacation visiting relatives, or something we've never done before?"

If you start adding more choices, then you are likely to end up in a state of indecision. It's like going to the supermarket and finding 38 different kinds of jam or breakfast cereal, which, if you don't already have a preference, can be overwhelming, so much so, that you come away with nothing. (If you do have a preference, put on your mental blinders so that you don't even see the alternatives.)

So back to the crucial question: "Would you rather go to a restaurant or see a movie first?" or the classic pick-up line, "Your place or mine?" if you're bold and into clichés.

I can't choose!

The problem of choice was the research project of Barry Schwartz (Schwartz, 2004). He found that if people were given too many options (more than a handful – sometimes three makes it hard!) they choose not to choose at all. It is often claimed – by politicians, especially – that what people want is more choice. But this is very often untrue. What they want is what they want, and that does not include the hassle of investigating the options and then trying to decide which best meets the need. Here's an opportunity for getting it wrong, and no one likes to think they made the wrong choice. When you do actually survey all the possible variations, you often find that no single one of them gives you all the things you want, so you have to make trade-offs. That means you miss out on something you thought was desirable, and so you feel bad and give up.

The joy of dating

When it comes to choosing friends and possible partners, we often find that other people are thrust upon us, so to speak.

During the trial period we give them the benefit of the doubt, and we wait and see what happens. If you are deliberately looking to find a particular kind of relationship using some kind of dating system, then you start with some kind of list of all the desirable features you think are important in a relationship. For example, your criteria may include good-looking, non-smoker, GSOH, and so on. When it comes to the crunch though, you meet someone to whom you are attracted – it's a case of chemistry, that indefinable something that produces a rush of hormones – and your list goes out of the window.

And don't think that compatibility is a valid search criterion. Like happiness, compatibility is a description you apply looking back at what you had – until it disappeared! So a dating system is good in that it gets you actively involved, but ultimately, it's not where it's at. It's more often the case that you meet someone, and you get a physiological response that tells you if it's worth going forward. It's not a rational decision that you can make with a list of pros and cons.

Think about the business of Speed Dating – or, as it's commonly known in business circles, Job Interviewing. The key factor is that you are presented with a person, with whom you have to establish some kind of rapport, and decide on the basis of flimsy, unreliable and unsubstantiated evidence whether this person will be good to have around and to work with. Sometimes it works well. During this brief interview period the emphasis is primarily on the instant relationship, a decision whether the other person is one of us (see Chapter 39). What's needed is in some kind of real-work activity where you can test out how you get along, whether you have made or are about to make the right decision.

That's how dating works – you give the other person (and yourself) a trial period, some kind of cooling-off period to allow the hormones to subside, so you can be a tad more objective and find out what it's like doing things together, and whether you could live with this. However, it is not always clear when this should finish, and there are frequent over-runs ...

Getting together

You're organizing a meal with friends, so it's sensible to plan ahead by drawing on your experience to imagine an ideal outcome. However, this may mean you fail to check in with your guests on what would be good for them. You reason, "Last time they were here we had lasagna, so we can't have that again," regardless of the fact that it was several months ago, and many dinners have been eaten during that time – and would they really remember? (People often do!) So you mentally run through the fish recipes you're good at. Then, what's for dessert? That chocolate number which they loved before (or at least they said they loved, but also hinted something about diets ...) So you contemplate something with fewer calories ... Get the picture? It's based on fear, and it's mind-reading on a grand scale. The reality is that your visitors have come to see you, and probably don't really mind what they eat. They are not restaurant critics; they just want a good time in your company. What they don't want is the host and hostess neurotically trying to meet some imaginary criteria of excellence which prevents them from being present and enjoying the company.

If this is something you're familiar with, what's it about? Do you fear being rejected ... and start playing low status to a bowl of pasta? The problem is that it's all going on in your mind and that shuts you off from your friends. You're wanting to do the best for your visitors but that only sets you off worrying about yourself. So what's the worst thing that can happen? You've probably already thought of this! No really. In your imagination, the soufflé doesn't rise, the vegetables are soggy, there's a smell of burning coming from the kitchen ... People matter more. Be there for them, not fretting over the fettuccine. They're resilient; they'll survive your screw ups. Of course it seems like a disaster at the time, but as long as it wasn't deliberate just realize you've had another opportunity to learn something from your poor performance: "That didn't go well, did it?" One day you'll look back on this and laugh ... so why wait? What happened is forgivable. After all, if you were the guest and it was your friends having the calamity – you'd understand, wouldn't you? So take a deep breath, and level with them. You can always order pizza. Put it down to experience – a memorable experience that brings a smile when you remember it. No big deal. You learned your lesson. And they're still your friends.

Fear of missing out or FoMO

Everybody has to be somewhere, but no one can be everywhere. There are always more interesting things going on where you aren't, and despite your mobile device showing you pictures of what you're missing, it just isn't the same. Wanting not to miss out can become something of a neurotic obsession. Commonly known as FoMO – Fear of Missing Out – can be distracting. You want to be here there and everywhere with all of your friends, and because you can't, you now feel failure approaching. Too many choices, so you're stymied, unable to decide what to do next. And your mind is buzzing so you're not even fully present – you're missing out on even more.

Life is full of examples. At large conferences there are times when specific interest sessions are run simultaneously and people split into small groups. Once I discovered that the people hosting a get-together they'd organized were anxious because there was now no way they could attend and listen in to every group. Plenaries were fine. But the fear was that they were going to miss out because they didn't have spies in every camp.

According to a survey conducted in the US and the UK, the majority of adult Millennials (age between 18 and 34) expressed that they want to say yes to everything due to the fear of missing out; over a half of the respondents said that they barely invest sufficient energy or time in delving into topics or new interests.

FEAR OF REJECTION • 133

(Wikipedia)

Some people are gadget junkies, and they have to have the latest whatever it is. iPhones come into this category; computer operating systems did once upon a time. Does this apply to you? Can you live without the newest and shiniest? Sure. You're not that bothered because yours works fine. You don't want the hassle of learning a new system, you're happy with the old way of doing things. And you have a policy of letting others go through the beta-testing and bug-removing period before you dip your toe in.

When you finally choose – to intervene, to buy, to leave a relationship – you may be left with the fear that you made the wrong decision. Because no one likes to admit they made a lousy choice – and at the time you don't know whether it was or not – you stave off feeling bad or uncertain by looking on the bright side. You twist your decision around and make it sound good. Accentuate the positive. This 'cognitive dissonance' is our way of coping and keeping our spirits up when we know, deep down, that we could have screwed up.

In the fullness of time, the truth comes out. The emotions have faded, all relevant factors have been considered and you can be honest with yourself. But there are still opportunities for worry: "If only I had done ..." "If only I'd known then what I know now." Sigh. Slump. Of course you can live your life like this, but wouldn't it be better to think of the benefit you derived from the decision you did make? Even if it turned out less than wonderful in the long run, you learned from that – didn't you?

Life in overdrive

One aspect of this fear is that you try to do as much as possible in the time available. However, that often results in doing many things not very well or doing so much that you are not fit company for the significant other in your life at the end of the day – or at the weekend, if you allow yourself to have one.

Check how you respond to these statements:
- I often think I can squeeze more than I really can into my day.
- I often spread myself too thin, for fear of missing out.
- I often only get to skim the surface of new interests, never having ample time or energy to truly delve deeply into the given topic or endeavor.
- I am overwhelmed by the amount of information I need to digest to stay up to speed.

There is so much more to know about these days, and this awareness is being pointed out to us on a regular and ubiquitous basis. In other words, there's no escape. So how does this make you feel? Depressed – indifferent – excited? If you've grown up in this kind of milieu then you may see it as normal. For us slightly older folk, who have seen tremendous changes over the last half century, we're a bit more laid back, only occasionally rising to the challenge of getting or having more. We take comfort from the saying, "In a hundred years this won't seem so important."

Cognitive dissonance

This is the mental stress or discomfort you get when you are holding two or more contradictory beliefs, ideas, or values at the same time. We often experience cognitive dissonance when we are confronted by new information that conflicts with how we thought things were. For example, you subscribe to reducing climate change, but still drive a gas-guzzling vehicle.

Leon Festinger (Festinger, 1957) put forward a theory to explain why people tended to resist changing:

> People tend to be consistent in their attitudes, beliefs and values. They will attempt to achieve 'congruence' between what they think and what they do. In a situation

where they have to choose between alternatives – all of which have both positive and negative features – there may be a feeling of conflict brought about by having to accept some undesirable features, and reject some desirable features in the alternatives.

Cognitive dissonance occurs when any new scientific research shows that previous thinking was wrong, or when the research debunks common urban myths. One famous case showed that the connection between autism and the MMR vaccine was based on faulty research methodology. And remember Mehrabian? Even though the numbers are erroneous, people like them and go on believing …

It may be difficult to understand someone's position when they continue to live in what to you is obviously an abusive relationship. How can she stay with that man? Somehow, the woman engages in a mental distortion that somehow makes it right. The justification may be based on the observation that relationships do go through bad patches; of disbelief: "I'm giving him the benefit of the doubt"; or fear of the unknown: 'Things could be worse …" (Murphy, 2012).

CHAPTER 22

Saying Yes

There are people who prefer to say "Yes," and
there are people who prefer to say "No." Those
who say yes are rewarded by the adventures they
have, and those who say "No" are rewarded by
the safety they attain.
~KEITH JOHNSTON, *Impro* p. 92

ONE OF YOUR FRIENDS, COLLEAGUES, or your partner suggests something. You have to decide Yes or No. It's your call. Hmm.

Every time you have to make a decision there's an element of discomfort because of the uncertainty, the cognitive dissonance. Should you stick with what you know, or should you trying something new and different? It's completely understandable that we learn caution. You recall those times you had your fingers burned because you were too trusting, so you pull into your shell and treat anything not vouched for by your friends as somewhat dubious, and probably to be avoided at all costs. The downside is that you may be missing out on what life has to offer, missing things that you would enjoy, derive pleasure from, learn from, and which would enhance your relationships with other people.

You might think that allowing the other person to make the decision for you would reduce your cognitive strain – the feeling that comes with indecision – but you still won't know if you made the best decision, or whether the alternative would have been better.

One way to get rid of doubt and uncertainty is to say Yes and go along with it. Then you can turn your attention outwards and focus on the upcoming experience. Of course there will be times when saying Yes will be unethical, immoral, illegal or downright stupid. You'll know when this is true – that small voice inside you nagging in the background. And it's not a good idea to say Yes to something that sounds too good to be true – there are many scammers out there ready to take you for a ride or to empty your bank account.

As long as personal safety is not an issue, trying saying Yes to suggestions more often, rather than automatically dismissing every offer put to you. Sure, this will take you out of your comfort zone, but that's no bad thing. You can go back there whenever you like. But think of the adventures you could be having. Think of the shared experiences, the discoveries you can make about yourself, and about other people – and the stories you'll be able to tell your friends later.

By saying yes to ideas, you may find yourself challenging your own imposed limits, constraints, beliefs – and beliefs always need challenging and updating because many of them are way past their expiry date. Even better, saying yes to other people's ideas is a great way to build relationships. This is where a bit of curiosity is a good thing. It's too easy to believe your version of reality, that your creative ideas are all important. By exploring and going along with other people's point of view you'll be developing versatility, which will trigger more ideas for you. It's all about making connections – both mentally and in relationships.

What's stopping you? How about all those "Yes, but ..." excuses for not doing something. Now you have an opportunity to define these blocks and remove them. So ask yourself: What is getting in the way of me doing X? What is that excuse all about? What am I trying to prevent happening? What's the fear?

Saying No

Sometimes it's not about fear, but overcoming inertia. If someone invites you to do something that is not part of your habitual routine, do you tend to say No and then find some excuse to justify it. It's too easy: saying No relieves you of the task of thinking about and evaluating alternatives. Be wary if this becomes your default setting: hankering for tradition, the status quo, the way it's always been and will be forever more ...

You look back at your personal history of interesting events and find it easy to feel fully justified for rejecting one opportunity which subsequently turned out a disaster. Or if you had said yes, then you would have missed out on something much more important. Or you said yes and came to regret making that decision, so never again: "It seemed a good idea at the time." Was that because you hadn't thought it through or put it in context?

You think first about your own need for comfort, not having to bother; you might consider these somewhat egocentric. You're thinking about yourself, not about what would please others. In other words, you're blocking. This could be a key factor in a project that goes off-track: you're getting in your own way. You are not trusting others or the process; you are part of the problem. The art is to recognize and then eliminate your personal sabotage. Because you are probably not aware of it consciously, you'll need to ask others in your family or in your team: What have they noticed that's getting in the way? What do I need to stop doing? So do that.

Reinventing yourself

What would your life be like if you were to challenge your supposed need for comfort and security? What if you were to remove those obstacles and seek out those things which could enhance your life? If a complete life-style change freaks you out, start with small adjustments. Recognize and celebrate what you have going for you. This is not the time for false modesty, self-effacement, or minimizing your talents. What are your special skills, knowledge, understanding? Think in fairly specific terms, rather than generalities. If your talent is for baseball, then are you a batter or a pitcher? If you enjoy photography, do you excel with landscapes or with portraits? Better to master what really appeals to you than try to be a jack of all trades. Then consider how you could use those particular skills to somehow complement someone else's abilities.

If you do something that you know is a minority interest, don't immediately assume that other people won't be interested. For example, if your major is in math, you may find that when you tell people that straight out, they will find an excuse to change the subject or move away. That's the problem with stating generalities. Instead, go for the benefit that it brings. For example, if you teach elementary school, start by talking about how you love working with young children and their infinite curiosity. Or turn it into a mystery to be solved: "Have you ever wondered how internet security is achieved?" This is a good way of grabbing their attention.

CHAPTER 23
"I'm Only Doing It For You"

WHEN OTHER PEOPLE MAKE DEMANDS on you: for your company, for your time, you have to decide how to respond. Do you come out with a clear yes or no, or do you seek further information: "Mmm, it depends ... Tell me more." There's a whole variety of situations in which it's not clear what to do in order to make a decision, so it might be a good idea to think through what motivates and influences you.

What is your primary motivation?

People and Gossip
It's time to catch up, renew contacts, acquaintanceships or to keep existing relationships going. It may not matter what you actually do – it's being with them that counts.

Position and Status
You need to be seen to be there, to maintain your position and status in the group. This applies to meetings (even the dreaded meetings) as well as significant events where, because of your role, you are there representing something or other and there is a strong expectation or obligation to show your face, if only for a brief period.

Personal and Altruistic
This is doing something that primarily benefits you by engaging in an activity in the company of others. This could be anything from playing in an orchestra to playing baseball – any kind of activity where the whole is greater than the sum of the parts – or being a volunteer helping others and at the same time providing you with useful work and good company.

Possibility and Opportunity
You want to do something new and different, because you're bored, because you're curious, and because you don't know where it may lead … and whom you might meet along the way.

One factor which may play a significant part in your decision is whether one person is asking you or whether the request is coming from a group. If it's a solitary person, then you have the opportunity to check their reasons for asking you. All the possibilities in the list above, and others, could apply. So decide what the objective is for getting together:

- An external event, such as a concert, the theatre, a sports match – something which has a scheduled place and time. Having a deadline helps you plan.
- A social gathering – a party, a celebration, a wedding or other social event.
- Hanging out: "We're going out and we'd like you to join us." The rather vague, poorly-defined outcome is to have fun or to be together. This can be a hard one to call – it depends on the alternatives, so you must base your decision on your current state and past experience.

Bowling in Baltimore
How many times have you done something you didn't really want to do or gone somewhere you didn't want to go? But, you did. Why? Because you wanted to be nice and please someone else. You probably didn't have strong feelings one way or the other so you deferred to someone else's preference. That's usually good for building relationships. But consider what happens when the other person is likewise indifferent. They are making suggestions they thought you'd like. Now you're in a mind-reading loop, going around in circles, each trying hard to please the other.

> "So, Jane, how about we drive into town, bowl a few lines, grab a beer and watch the game?"
> "Sure. That sounds great."

Off they go. Later that evening, there's some silent tension between Jane and Bob.

> "You OK, Jane?" says Bob.
> "No, not really" says Jane with a certain chill to her voice.
> "Why not, honey?"
> "You've forgotten how much I hate the noise, the smoke ... not to mention the pain from my broken toe from the last time I dropped the ball on my foot!"
> "Then why did you say yes?!"
> "I don't know, I just thought you'd like to go."

Bob was attempting to please Jane. Jane was trying to please Bob. But they failed to get agreement over what they wanted to do. They both gave in, failed to stand up for what they really wanted in order to make the other feel good. The result: two unhappy and disappointed people who are a bit angry. This is known as the Abilene Paradox. It's not a failure to agree, it's a failure to disagree, to stand up for what you want. If Jane had said,

> "Thanks for the suggestion, hon, but I'd rather not. I really don't like the noise and the smoke … and remember my toe still hurts when ever we drive by the bowling alley. How about we get some snacks, invite Judy and George over, and watch the game here?

Now it has become a negotiation. Each person is talking from a position of strength, rather than trying to avoid displeasure. So before you blithely succumb to group pressures, you need to check out other people's expectations.

It's often the case that groups exert more pressure than an individual. Nor is it so easy to fathom the real intention behind the offer. If you are being asked or even pressured by a group, it may seem easier to give in to what you think they want rather than assert your individuality. If the plan is to have fun – as in the last alternative, then you may probably experience some internal conflict: part of you wants to be with kindred souls, while another part could do with a quiet moment or time to get on with all those things you've been putting off.

In more formal or official contexts, there will be certain expectations and obligations put on you. You have officially joined a company, an organization, a team, a work-group; to some extent, you are expected to conform to some kind of rules: "The way we do things" – the company style, ritual behaviors, and so on. Could mean going for a drink after work, or going to the boss's garden party. There are consequences for not attending, for not conforming – you are ostracized, even asked to leave, and ignored or passed over on future occasions (if you don't have a good excuse this time).

The Abilene Paradox

So why this name for the human trait of "I'm only doing this to please you"? It's a paradox in that people end up voting for what they *don't* want; they reach an agreement about what to do but no one actually wants to do it. It's easy to fall into this paradox if you try to please other people by thinking you know what they would like (see "The Problem with Mind-reading" in Chapter 20).

The story comes from an article published in 1974 by management expert Jerry B. Harvey (Harvey, 1988). You really need to read the original to get the full flavor of the incident that gave its name to this phenomenon. There's a summary on Wikipedia which has the essence.

Briefly:

> On a hot Texas afternoon, the family is comfortably playing dominoes. The father-in-law suggests they go to Abilene [53 miles north] for dinner. The wife says, "Sounds great." The husband, despite reservations, thinks his preferences are out-of-step with the group and says, "Sounds good to me. I just hope your mother wants to go." The mother-in-law then says, "Of course I want to go. I haven't been to Abilene in a long time."
> The drive is hot, dusty and long. Arriving at the cafeteria, the food is as bad as the drive. They arrive back home four hours later, exhausted.
>
> One says ironically, "Great trip, wasn't it?" The mother-in-law says that, actually, she would rather have stayed home, but went along since the others were so enthusiastic. The husband says, "I only went to satisfy the rest of you." The wife says, "I just went along to keep you happy. I was crazy to go out in that heat." The father-in-law says he only suggested it because he thought the others might be bored.
>
> The group realizes that together they decided to take a trip which none of them wanted. Each would have preferred to stay put, but did not admit to it when asked.

The result of this kind of thinking is that everyone ends up worse off than if they'd done nothing. Therefore, it is worth considering who is making suggestions, based on their known history for caring about others. In other words, do these people consistently want to please, and say things like "I thought you'd like this" or "I'm only doing this for you"? If so, then a different tactic is required. Mounting a direct inquiry "Is this what you really want?" could be seen as an attack; those in power might consider that you've stopped being a team-player and are showing disloyalty to the group. So again, use some softeners:

"I'm wondering if this is such a good idea. Perhaps we could think it through before we make a firm decision." If you have support from the others, ask: "Will it work? Does it make sense? Does it fit with our company policy? Is it worth the time and effort? Is it legal, moral, ethical?" It helps if the other people know about the Abilene paradox, because then you can short-cut the process by asking "Are we going to Abilene?"

Knowing that people act the opposite to their beliefs, be on the lookout for Abilene situations. The Abilene paradox can appear in different contexts – especially in the work environment when bosses or leaders do not like having their decisions challenged. Perhaps you know people like this. If so, you don't cross them, at least not directly. You could switch to the multiple option strategy, which gives people an alternative to simply caving in to pressure: "If I may suggest that we could be limiting our options here … we could be missing a trick if we don't consider …" But if you're up against a dictator … well, do you have to stay there?

In terms of group or family dynamics, stating your position on an issue or decision, saying what you don't want and exploring a range of options instead of thinking "There's only one way to do this", will bring you closer to other team or family members because you are encouraging them to say where they are at. Opening up increases the information you have – not only about options, but also about individual's preferences and desires. It's always far better to be operating from a position of more information rather than from guesswork and assumptions.

CHAPTER 24
Agreements and Disagreements

Right and Wrong

How easy it is to disagree. It all depends on your point of view:

I'm objective; you're biased.

I'm right; you're wrong, misguided, devious.

I have evidence to support my views; you just don't
know how to interpret it correctly.

My overall aim is perfection; yours is to frustrate and
confuse.

TRUTH AND LIES
It's frequently claimed that everyone tells lies to some
extent. I would of course deny this, but then you would
probably accuse me of lying. There's no such thing as the whole
truth; every truth is partial. It's your version, your story of what
happened. No two witnesses to an event ever completely agree.
Remember this when you are having a battle of interpretation.
Instead of digging in, inquire how the other person sees things,
because they will have different biases from you and this may
throw new light on the situation.

People tell what are called white lies in order to conceal an
inconsequential detail of their activities – they don't want to, or
don't have the time, to explain what they have been doing. They
could be editing one of their stories to boost their status (see
Chapter 10). Or they may resort to euphemism in order to spare
the other person potential upset or bad feeling. For example, if
you are asked for a comment on something they have done or
acquired, then it's possible to be neutral in the face of a hideous
ornament or garish garment: "Wow!" works. "That's making
a statement." Were you to say what you really think, stating it

honestly and bluntly, then, should it strike home, it could be quite hurtful. We have a tendency to build protective bubbles around ourselves that are meant to insulate us from harmful information. People do not like having their bad choices or flaws pointed out. They might be suffering from buyer's remorse or pretending that no one else has noticed.

On the other hand, if you are really seeking feedback on your choices or on what you have done, because you want to know how to improve, then simply being told "That's nice" is unhelpful. You want a range of objective honest opinions because these will give you something to work on.

Honesty is the best policy … until it's not. When is it appropriate to lie to someone with whom you want to build a relationship? One of the marital arts is knowing when to be vague, when to be kind, when to stay silent. Everyone is beautiful in their own way, so tell them, "How beautiful you look." Actually, telling other people how good, clever, positive they are, will actually have them live up to these descriptions – they actually become better, more positive and so on. Their beauty increases according to that inner glow they get from a compliment.

How shall I put this?
Sometimes a quick dose of honesty relieves us of further problems later on. Suppose you notice something about another person that is not that flattering, something they are unaware of (for example, the booger hanging from their nose, their offensive body odor or their inappropriate misogynistic humor). You need to overcome any embarrassment, and pass on information in a neutral kind of way: "Did you know that ...?" so that they can use this information to immediately remedy the situation. They'll probably be grateful you told them. But if it's an annoying habit, or just their way of relating to others, then you have to consider whether your intervention will hurt the relationship. Do you want to protect them from harm or

cause them harm? Do you want to condone their inappropriate behavior, or do you want to point it out so that they become aware of what's happening?

We often excuse annoying characteristics of those whom we like or love thinking they will change over time. When they don't change, we add to the store of harmful or negative information that we can use against them in some future fight. Of course, there's nothing compulsory about this. Those who have the most positive relationships either reveal this information to the other person in confidence, in private, when there is no conflict around or they refuse to use this information ... ever.

"It's Fine." Dealing with Passive-Aggressive behavior

The wheels of conversation do not always turn smoothly. There will be times when you want to know what's going on, but you're being stone-walled. You're getting nothing back from the other person; they are engaging in what is known in the trade as passive-aggressive behavior – they're being polite, but not giving anything away. They are refusing to talk to you, essentially. So you begin to wonder: Is it me? Is it something I've done, or not done? What's going on here? Perhaps it's them? Are they just in a mood? Alas, it's not always easy finding the answers.

Passive-aggressive behavior is when someone is directing their anger, resentment, hostility towards another person, convinced that they will know what it's all about. Typically you get the mind-reading accusation, "You know what the matter is. I'm not going to spell it out!" But they don't make the actual problem clear. Perhaps it's because they feel they're being treated unfairly, being humiliated, ridiculed, put down or undervalued in a situation for the umpteenth time.

The visible evidence of such behavior is ambiguous; maybe they give the appearance of sweetness and light, but underneath it all there's hostility. Because it doesn't make sense, there's no clear response you can make. The result is a feeling of upset and discomfort. Because you can't understand what's happened, closure is not possible; you enter a state of mental limbo. Trouble is, this may be exactly what the other person wants! It's their way of getting at you; they have the upper hand.

On the domestic front, when you're on the receiving end: "How could you?!", implies "You should know better!" This is followed by silence or rejection, and you're in the doghouse for breaking one of your partner's rules, but you're not sure which one. Arguing is not a good option. It may mean waiting till the storm blows itself out. Or you may try an intervention, "Hon, can we talk about this?" Could work.

When you feel you are the one slighted, it's a natural response to retaliate. So you find a way of subtle sabotage, intending to inflict some psychological or emotional damage on the other person, in the vague hope that they will see sense, understand your problem, change their behavior … Dream on. Yes, it is rather childish, but what can you do when your status has been lowered. You feel like dirt, so you play dirty. That makes sense? Probably not on the domestic front. It's not going to improve things. However, you can probably get away with it in a business setting. You're filling in the time while you look for another position, another company, so you need to play nice in order to get a good reference. You're not going to do anything that can be proved to be a misdemeanor, nothing that breaks the rules, nothing that invites official sanctions or warnings. You're treading a fine line, finding ways of delaying, ignoring, missing appointments, bad-mouthing the other person behind their back, or writing anonymous insults using social media. Or you could go the official route and work to rule. And so on – human ingenuity is boundless in such situations.

What to do instead? This is a bit like 'I don't know'; you have to admit to yourself "I've been hurt." Forget those childhood injunctions about "Big boys and girls don't cry." Crying is a good way of dealing with hurts – you cry, you feel better, and you take positive action to put things right. You need a grown-up version that lets you do this. But do it in private; don't make a public display.

The Art of Nothing

You want to know, so you ask: "What are you doing?" You use a neutral kind of voice; you're not the Spanish Inquisition. "Nothing." Another ambiguous answer, a blocking response. Were you just being nosy, or do you think you are entitled to know? Obviously you are at cross purposes here. Similarly, when you notice the other person is upset or emotionally disturbed, you want to help, if possible. But when you ask: "What's the matter?" you get a "Nothing" or "I'm fine. It's OK." Again, you have to decide whether or not to follow that up. One possibility is that they come back to you high status, and treat you as the one with the problem: "Don't *you* worry about it" "Well, I am worried." "Well, don't be." This goes nowhere.

If you can get a handhold into their world, you can begin to change the situation. Although they are offering you nothing, you can work with that. Dare to ask, "So what kind of nothing is that?" This is not a common response, and I've never heard it used in any Hollywood movie, even though it would often enliven many an otherwise dull script. It creates a swift refocus of attention – sometimes enough to shock them out of the mood they're in, just in order to answer the question. That could be enough. They've made a change. And there's no need to do or say anything else.

So when you are being given the brush-off, the question you have to ask yourself is, "How important is it for me to know?" If you did know, what would you do then? Would it make a difference? Would it be a matter of life or death? Are you ready for anything they might say? Because knowing would affect what you do and your response to them. And if you never know, what would be the worst that could happen? Whatever you do, don't go in high status – you're not their therapist or boss. It's all about sensitivity in reading body language, and acting at the appropriate level. So you explain, "I really am worried about you. You're not your usual self. I'm concerned." You may get the response, "Never mind." Sometimes you just can't get through.

CHAPTER 25
Dealing With Criticism

THE OPPOSITE OF PASSIVE-AGGRESSIVE IS in-your-face criticism. Being criticized is always tough; you're under attack, regardless of how nice the other person is being, however they dress it up. They are suggesting that in some way you should alter yourself, your behavior, your work of art, your business report – to make it conform more closely to their standards, which are naturally higher than yours.

Although your critics might say they're doing it for your own good, that is probably not the case. Most criticism is a kind of put-down, implying that whatever it was you did was not good enough, plain wrong, or punishable by death. Just kidding. The trouble is, in our blame culture, this strategy doesn't work. The intention is to produce a change. The reality is that you hear the negatives, defend yourself, dig in and resist further advice.

Criticism especially doesn't work when you enter the realms of absolutism. This is when you start criticizing someone else, perhaps your beloved (because then you can draw on years of experience), making "You ..." statements, such as "You're always doing *x*" or "You never do *y*." This is over-generalizing with words such as *always* and *never* – which are exaggerations and unlikely to be true. So they put up the barriers and then start lobbing counter-accusations at you. Is this the essence of marital conflict? Could be. Once the other person has blocked you, there is nothing going to go in. Further feedback is a waste of time, and of breath, and another step along the path of relationship breakdown.

If you are on the receiving end and are able to stay open

to what is being thrown at you, you'll find that this kind of communication may have some objective truth but is more often likely to be manipulative or representative of your accuser's unmet needs. What comes across is a mish-mash of their beliefs, values, emotional responses together with some elements of a BFO (blinding flash of the obvious) – things you probably know and agree with and may have already decided to do something about. When it comes to effective communication, this is not it. The way to deal with criticism is to separate the person from the problem – this is Fisher and Ury's *Getting to Yes* strategy (Fisher & Ury, 1981). What it means in practice is careful listening, isolating the specific event being referred to from the background of frustration, anger, or contempt. Elsewhere in the book I mention the idea of putting the contentious issue out there in that neutral space in front of you both so that you can be more objective in dealing with it. Body language makes a difference. Standing face-to-face plants the issue directly on the other person. That's why you need to turn and stand side-by-side. Then you can deal with it together.

Once you're in a safe discussion situation – that is, you've calmed down and are ready to share the process of examining how things could be different – you need to be clear about how you ask questions. No "why did you…?" accusations about past behavior. The focus now is on your interests, what you want for the future. Treat this as if you have been called in to sort out someone else's problem; you are just investigators who are digging down to get to the underlying causes and to reach some possible solutions. When you have a reasonably clear idea of what's happened, what the plan was, and what deviations occurred, then find out the part you have to play in future: "What's one thing I could do to improve this/to stop this happening again?" You need a clear, doable answer, something you can implement right away (see Chapter 15).

For example, if it's about the way you say things, such as your tendency to use 'you' statements, try out a sentence along the lines of "I feel neglected when you spend three evening a week out with your team-members" (as opposed to "You're always out in the evenings"). If it's a practical thing, do it now; if it means taking out the garbage, well, you know how to do that.

If you don't know or are unsure how to make the change, ask "How do you think I could do that? Could you assist me or let me know when I'm getting it right?" You might want to clarify the criteria as well: "How would I know I was getting it right, in your eyes?" – because when things become OK for the other person, they also become invisible.

"You could be right"

Sometimes you feel other people are accusing you of things which you think are unjust, irrelevant, or more to do with them than with you. If you don't want to go down the route of sorting things out – you don't see what's in it for you – then another tactic is to go bland and neutral. You're not going to change; you just want them off your back.

First of all, find a way of agreeing with the criticism. They are probably wound up and wanting an argument, but you're not going to give them that pleasure. You disarm them by agreeing: "You could be right." "You may have a point there." The next move is theirs, but in a sense they've already won. Where to go? If you feel you are being wronged, this may seem a challenge, but there should be some grain of truth in what your critic says that you can recognize. Antagonism is not usually a good ploy.

So, for example, your critic says, "You're spending far too much time watching sports on the television, and I'm getting really pissed off because you're not doing your share around the house." There is obviously a problem for them here, but you're not yet sure what it is. But rather than immediately getting into a blazing fight by contradicting anything, find the bit you can agree on. "Yes, I do watch a lot of sports on TV." This shows the critic that they have been heard, they have been validated – to a degree. But you have not given them any holds, so it's back to them to make the next move. Your job is to keep quiet. You do not need to defend yourself, find excuses, or try to justify your behavior.

There are three ways of doing this.

- *Agree in part.* If the criticism has been stated in terms of absolutes such as *always, never, every time,* and so on – a device people use for exaggerating when they are pissed off – then go vague so that you are not contradicting them but offering a bland general statement. "Yes, I do watch a lot of sports on TV." Avoid the 'around the house' part, because that's a different issue and one that needs to be carefully debated.
- *Agree in probability.* Use words such as *might, could, may* which suggest that something might be the case, but imply nothing about your particular situation. Construct some sentences along the lines of "You could be right" or "You may have a point there," which kind of validates the critic, but makes no connection with you.
- *Agree in principle.* If the critic has suggested some consequences of your action, in the form of an 'if … then …" statement, then agree with it. You're still in generality land. Something along the lines of "I agree. If I were to watch TV all day, I'd never get the garden dug."

Getting the details

When they have calmed down, you want to get to the bottom of this so you need to ask your critic some questions that will clarify, for both of you, what exactly the issue here is. In asking questions, you are pushing responsibility back on the other person – what's *their* problem? – so that in order to move forward they have to pinpoint the real issue – which gave rise to them criticizing you in the first place.

Pick what you see as a key part of their message, and frame a question along the lines of "What is it about *x* that bothers you?" or "So what is it about *x* that you want to be different?" In this case, "What is it about me watching sports that bothers you?" or "What is it about my way of doing things around the house that you would like to change?"

Tell me More

You could just be curious, or you could see this as a delaying tactic. By saying, "Tell me more", you are not yet ready to make your response; you want more information, especially about how they see the situation. In a sense you are agreeing to enter their world – which flatters them. You are showing an interest and at the same time subtly challenging what they said initially. The ball's in the speaker's court; they are prompted to take a moment to think about and expand on what they have just said. There's a sense that we always know that what we say is not the whole truth, always an approximation of it.

"Tell me more" is relatively neutral – if said in a neutral voice, with a hint of genuine curiosity.

"That sounds interesting … Tell me more." The speaker then needs to justify, explain, explore or define what they're getting at. They may give the background story of what concerns them or give you an idea of their plan or intention (or they could decide they don't want to go there and give up).

By going into more detail, they are also informing themselves, and this information may be new to them. It might even upset the status quo because they are now questioning for themselves. This is the point of such an intervention. How you respond matters, because you have the choice of changing the game or of escalating the situation, which is probably not in your best long-term interest. For example, you are:

- Defusing anger, aggression or resentment. Slowing things down, taking a breath, a moment to think things through. "Well ..." pause. "I don't know about you ..."
- Diverting or deflecting the other person's attention. "I'm wondering ..." "What particularly are you concerned about ...?"
- Lowering your status: "I'm confused here ..." "I'm sorry, it's me. I don't understand ..."

These and other similar tactics have the effect of changing the other person's mental and emotional state, and this adjustment enables you to focus on something more productive than a ding-dong battle. No longer are you a victim under attack or an object of derision. You have become more of a partnership working to resolve a problem, a rational human being doing your best to get along with other people.

CHAPTER 26
Planning

"If you want to make God laugh, show him your plans."

WHAT DO YOU WANT FROM a relationship? It's a tough question to answer for most of us, simply because we do not know what will happen in the future. People, especially, seem to be unpredictable. The default value is to assume things will be very much the same as before. Given that all our efforts are directed at trying to change the world – and other people – in some way, we can't take anything for granted. Planning is relatively easy when it's something you've done before – building a house, designing a garden, organizing a vacation – but when it comes to planning relationships, people either don't know what they want or expect because they haven't thought about it, or they're keeping their options open and playing their cards close to their chest.

Although many relationships just bumble along, there are times when you do need to do some planning. This is obvious when you're just beginning a new personal relationship, when you want to get things right – you don't want to upset or turn the other person off – and you certainly want to ensure you come across as a likable and sensible person.

Your planning skills also come into play when you notice that things are starting to go wrong or off-track, whether this is at the beginning or well into a long-term relationship. For example, an element of unhappiness has crept into a relationship and it's causing you or your partner grief. Some kind of intervention is required. You need to think about where you are heading and make a plan, and that includes telling the other person what you are thinking. They need to know and recognize that something needs to be done. They may have been keeping quiet, hoping things would go away or get better on their own. But that's not always going to happen. Left alone, situations usually get worse.

Part of the problem may be that it's difficult to make plans together especially if one person is insisting on a particular point of view and won't budge. One way around this is to go back to first principles: why are you in this relationship at all? What did you hope was going to happen when you got together? There must have been some clear intention, though it may have gone unsaid to some degree. OK, it's easy to say "Let's get married" without getting specific about what you think that entails. Unless you ask your partner – which may seem a bit weird to them – you could end up with very different ideas about what living together will mean in practice, in everyday life. Now could be the time to get clear about what you had hoped for – and to compare that with what seems to be happening now. So what does each of you want? How do you want the relationship to be in the future?

Start with the big picture: your dreams, ideals, what would bring you the most satisfaction from sharing a life together? Once you're clear on these (and it may be worth writing them down somewhere, so that you can remind yourself when things get busy) it's time to get into the details: How exactly do you propose to achieve these things? And what is getting in the way? Actually, the key pieces to the puzzle are these blocks, the negatives that are getting in the way. You need to be aware of whatever is coming between you and then do something about. Like, stop doing it, change your focus of attention, do more things that will meet the expectations of your partner.

So you each draw up a list of things to do more and things to do less of. Making explicit your joint plans is another aspect that possibly brings you closer – unless you find that you are violently disagreeing about what you want. If that's the case, then thinking in terms of the big picture is worth doing. It is sometimes the case that you will find vast discrepancies when you only look at the details of your individual short-term goals. Then you need to chunk up, to think in more general terms.

Although this has been framed in terms of a marriage relationship, it could easily apply to any kind of relationship in which you are on good enough terms to talk *about* the relationship itself. There are multitude of ways in which people differ on how the communicate, how they tackle the business of making sense of the world and other people, so a good attitude is to accept this and to be curious about "How do you do that?" Others might think your question is stupid if they think, "Well, doesn't everyone do this?" because the answer to that is No they don't. So you might need to explain this and describe your particular likes and dislikes here.

This is yet another way in which we're asking you to pay more attention to differences rather than blame the other person for being dumb or difficult. So before you respond negatively, simply stop doing whatever, and realize there's a mismatch. Rather than blame other people for being different or difficult, take it upon yourself to be responsible for making the communication work. That means you will have to find greater flexibility in the way you do things. It's good practice to cover the big picture as well as the details, the linear story as well as the pieces. Either adapt to their way of doing things or get curious and explore what these differences are. In other words, go in low status, willing to learn and improve. This is a good way of enhancing the various relationships you are in.

CHAPTER 27
Understanding Problems

Never try to teach a pig to sing; it wastes your
time and it annoys the pig.
~ PAUL DICKSON

YOU DON'T UNDERSTAND
When it comes to making sense of everyday life, we
frequently make the mistake of thinking we understand
other people, why they do what they do, and how they will feel
as a consequence. We think, "Well, if I were in their shoes, I'd
..." or "If that were happening to me, I'd feel ..." We mainly do
this by projecting our understanding and feelings onto them –
after all, it's a useful reference point. But the fact is that other
people are not us; they think and act in different ways and for
different reasons. Knowing why someone does what they do
is often a tricky thing to figure out. Very often, we don't really
know ourselves why we're doing what we do: is it a hangover
from our past, or an attempt to fulfill some long-held dream. We
don't know. We just do it.

Sure, you can see the faults another person demonstrates. A
fault is simply something they do that is not the way you do it.
Sure, they're flawed, because they are not as perfect as you. But
that does not give you the right to try and change them to meet
your high standards. So when you notice that you have the ideal
answer to all their problems ... Hold back. Resist. Don't try this
at home. Because it's the sure way to frustration, misery and
soured relationships.

What not to do
OK. So your relationship is having problems, what should you

do and not do? Trying to change the other person while still in the relationship does not have a high probability of success. Remember your status. Playing therapist means going high-status and commenting on the other person's behavior from a holier-than-thou point of view. If you promote yourself to be the expert on this relationship and suggest to your partner: "We need to go to relationship counseling," then what comes across to the other person is that you have just lowered their status. They interpret your suggestion as telling them, "You're a loser." They see your attempt at resolution as a way to fix them (not yourself – which is where they see the problem) and reject your intervention. As such, it's pretty much a waste of time, and could possibly make things worse.

Level the playing field. Admit to yourself that you don't have the answer. (If you did, then you probably wouldn't be in this predicament in the first place.) Lower your status, and become a genuinely concerned inquirer. "I'm not sure what's going on here, and it's obvious that both of us are feeling hurt." Get agreement. "I'd like to do something about it. So could you tell me how it is with you, how you see things?" This is one of the possible ways that could lead to opening up a dialogue between you. It's far more likely to be productive than simply jumping in with what you would do or think. First you need to establish the parameters, and that includes finding out what the other person is wanting from you.

Solving vs. Supporting

Bob's wife came home one day obviously stressed out. She was on the verge of tears, wearing a distressed facial expression. You know what I mean. Bob, wanting to be helpful, asked what was up. As she was explaining the issues, Bob jumped in periodically with suggestions for solutions. "If I were you, I woulda ..." She would stop, not respond, then start up with the explanation again. When Bob was done, and so proud of his helpfulness, he was a bit surprised by her continued anger, which was now directed at Bob. "Why are you angry at me?" he shouted. "I'm not the one who set your office on fire!" Now, they were both angry. "What did I do?" Bob said loudly.

Well, Bob tried to solve a problem that didn't concern him. One that the other person didn't really want his help in dealing with. All they wanted was a supportive shoulder that would allow them to dump their feelings and thoughts out into the open air. Bob's intentions were pure, but his actions only made matters worse.

Can you help me?
If people come to you with their problems, it's because they know that you will give them time, and will listen to what they have to say. That may be sufficient for them to sort things out. For them, 'letting it out' is part of the process of resolution. When they start to talk about whatever is bothering or upsetting them, for you it's like coming in at the middle of the story. Unless you know their history, it could take a moment for you to orient yourself into their reality and make sense of what they are saying. Or it could be that it doesn't matter what they are saying, because they are really talking to themselves, in their own private language. You are just a sounding board, there for moral support and to witness their process.

In situations like this, it is important to determine what kind of responses your significant other is looking for from you. Do they actually want your help providing solutions to the problem from your perspective? Or do they really just want you to nod your head and say, "That sounds awful," "What happened, what did you do?" "Is there anything you need from me?"

Don't laugh. This actually happened to me. My wife is a senior executive at an international firm, and a psychologist, just like me. One day after coming home, I could tell she was brooding and angry at the events of the day. I was thinking to myself,

"Do I offer a supportive shoulder and provide gentle nods and sympathetic expressions or do I tell her what I'd do." I thought that if she catches me trying to be empathetic (after all, she's a psychologist and knows all these tricks just as well as I do), she'll bite my head off. Then I thought that it was worth the risk to say, "Looks like you had a stressful day. Wanna talk about it?" Then I patiently held my breath, continued to make eye contact with her, and waited. In my head, my body position was defensive with my hands up ready for a fight. To my surprise, my wife opened up to me and proceeded to unload the burdens of her day. I would occasionally say, "That sounds terrible", "Wow" or "What did you do/think?" Afterwards she said "Thanks for listening. I feel much better." As I sat there quietly, somewhat stunned, still with the empathetic head tilt in place, I realized that I had made a breakthrough – for me. In the past, I prided myself on being a problem solver, a doer, a getter-done kinda guy. But, here I was, solving a problem without making a suggestion.

Later on that evening, we talked about the earlier conversation and she told me that sometimes she just needed to vent. Then we made an agreement that from now on, when one of us was stressed out, we would ask the other person what part they wanted us to play: to be a problem solver and jump in with helpful suggestions, or to be a listener, available to provide the support the other person is looking for at the moment. This was a learning experience for me.

"I'm lost"
Some people tend to silently follow a train of thought for quite a way before announcing some important conclusion, without giving any clue as to what has gone before. They think your bewilderment is uncalled for: "You should know what I'm talking about." Mind-reading rides again. "Sorry, I'm lost. Would you mind telling me ...?" So they run through when, where, what and with whom. This may be irritating or seen as

time-wasting by your speaker, but you need to know where this one-sided conversation is going, if anywhere.

Not knowing, being ignorant does not make you stupid (unless you're really trying hard). If you do need to understand the background of their story, then you will need to ask some questions for clarification – but only if knowing really matters. They already know; sometimes your nosiness is irrelevant. Although people like to be asked to explain, this may be getting in the way of them telling their story. So put yourself on hold for a while as you gather more details. When the other person has run out of steam, then is a good time to go in and clarify the details – if necessary. On the other hand, having to make an effort to put two and two together will mean you're more likely to be engaged and to remember their story. Wait and see if the essential clues are provided. Again, you're playing low status. Don't try to be clever. If the other person thinks you are stupid by asking dumb questions, being deliberately obtuse or trying to trip them up … You aren't, are you?! If eventually you fail to reach an Ah-ha moment, then you need to ask. Say "No. I really want to understand this from your point of view." Actually, being confused yourself probably reflects some of their confusion, and by asking questions, you're doing them a favor. Essentially, what you need to know is why they see this as a problem. In other words: What is it they want to do – but can't? What do they want to be different in some way?

So ask: "How is this a problem for you?" Don't be satisfied with the first answer you get. A problem usually involves a chain of stuff – some of it out of conscious awareness – and you need to dig down in order to find out what it is they really want to achieve. Problems are often the visible part of some deeper unease. There's a high probability that the context is important: "Is this a one off, or does this happen all the time? Does this occur generally or only in certain places or at specific times?"

It's useful to have the focus of *What do you want?* or *"How do you want things to be different?"* It's easy for them to forget to explain this, because they may not have thought things through themselves … yet. So, once you've got a handle on what's bugging them, turn the spotlight on what they want to change. Keep the focus on them; don't let them start talking about other people and things they can't change directly. "What do *you* want to achieve?" "And if you got that, what would it enable you to do that you can't do now?" or "What would that do for you?" "What would be the downside of getting what you want?" And then: "So is this feasible? Is it realistic?"

When you have gathered enough information to provide sufficient texture to their story, summarize what they have said to show to them and yourself that you understand something of what this is all about. "You know we were discussing the planting arrangement in the garden the other day, and you said there was a problem with drainage …" or "I've been thinking about what you said about the vacation and how this conflicts with your parents' anniversary …" This ties in with the other person's experience and enables you to continue. You may need to do a recap of the content: "We thought we could take out the lawn, and put in vegetables. Have you had any further ideas about this?"

It's important to remember that even though someone might think the problem is unique to them, that's highly unlikely. In reality, you're not the first to have this problem, and given the current trend in publishing everything online, you'll usually find someone else who has written about the problem and others who have offered solutions. As long as you treat such answers with care and a touch of skepticism and do whatever is suggested in a safe context, you should learn something useful.

Another approach, based on the age-old rule for malfunctioning devices, is to switch it off or unplug it, and then switch it on again. OK for technology, but with people? Sure. This is more than just a metaphor. You're in the middle of a heated monologue that you've heard before and know it's not going anywhere. So switch off, unplug, stop. Say "Stop!" and put your hands up, palms facing the situation. Just "Stop!" No need to explain or justify, although "I need a moment" might help. And then do something different. Anything, as long as it's different. Take your moment. Take another moment. Take a walk round the block. Anything that helps the person get some separation from the burning issue. You could physically guide them to take a step back – both literally or mentally – so that they gain some distance and a new perspective. Have them look hard at what's there, what's going on. What do they notice now? Then begin the process of reconnecting.

CHAPTER 28
Commitment

"**I**S YOU IS OR IS you ain't my baby?"
What does commitment mean to you? Does it suggest some kind of exclusivity agreement that is going to limit your freedom to be who you are? Quite often, the word 'commitment' sends shivers down the spines of men – more so than with women. Why? Well, women need commitment during the period of raising their children, and that's a relatively long time. For men, though, it somehow seems to dent their pride because they want to feel free to change their focus, to explore options, to attain the unattainable (and you have a pretty good idea of what that is!). It's a macho thing.

When you are getting closer to someone and you experience their desire for commitment to you, how do you feel? Wary? A desire to run away and hide; afraid of the consequences of long-term commitment? Or do you embrace this desire to be together for as long as possible … perhaps for a lifetime?

The reality is that most human beings, both women and men, actually do seek commitment. One reason is that people do not thrive very well in isolation from others; being in a couple is actually good for your health. Another reason is that it provides a secure base for living. It offers the promise of becoming part of a creative relationship in which you both do better than you would on your own. And as a couple you are treated as such and get invited to more dinner parties.

How do you identify yourself to strangers? "I'm John's wife" or "I'm Penny's other half." See? We often define ourselves in relation to others: that's who we are. Although we start off quite different people, over time we begin to shift towards a merged identity. In the same way, we do this with our friends and acquaintances, because we find it agreeable to be more alike than different. Over time we even begin to resemble, behave, and sound like each other, able to finish our partner's sentences.

We choose to affiliate with like-minded people, others of a similar ilk. It's comfortable; requires less work. We're basically tribal in nature; knowing and sharing the needs, wants and desires of the group helps us work in harmony with the others. The level of commitment varies with the group we belong to. We commit to a variety of groups and causes by giving time, money or support. Commitment is actually a sliding scale. Acute commitment is shorter term, ad hoc, temporary; chronic commitment is what is sought in long-term relationships like marriage and friendships. What you are looking for is balance over time.

In the process of joining a group may involve some kind of formal ritual. (More on this in Chapter 39.) Even if becoming a member is informal, then there is often an underlying assumption that you will devote a certain amount of your energy towards the overall success of the group. In other words, every relationship implies a degree of commitment.

Commitment is a way of expressing loyalty to a person or a group. That means you put them first when making a significant decision that affects both you and them. However, commitment does not mean that you annihilate yourself or become a doormat for the others, nor does it mean you have to devote yourself solely to one other person, nor sever your contact with other friends. If a partner or group insists that you do this, head for the door. You can be committed to many individuals and groups. Within your circle of friends and colleagues, each gets a share of your loyalty and commitment. The important thing is that part of the respect you have for others means having no secrets, that it is OK for everyone to know of the others' existence.

Being committed to a single person in a marriage scenario does not preclude either party from being committed to other short-term obligations. But if one party feels that the balance has been tilted too far to one side, that's where priority setting comes in helpful as a tool for re-setting a shaky relationship. Setting limits, goals and timelines and committing to their completion builds trust which in turn leads to deeper commitment. You need to do what you said you were going to do. If for some unforeseen reason you can't comply, then tell the other person ahead of time so that there are no surprises. It's those kinds of surprises that put immense pressure on relationships.

Commitment is a two-way street. If you are committed to someone else, do they reflect that back with equal strength? If they do not, this is a warning: why are they not committed to you? What else is going on? Relationships fall apart when one person is committed to the other but that commitment is not reciprocated. It is natural, however, that commitments are never at the same level in any relationship at the same time. They are stronger at some points and weaker at others depending on what other factors are on the minds of the people involved. "You spend all your time down at the club! I'd like a piece of your time too, ya know!" shouts a wife in frustration. The husband is torn between wanting to be with his wife and also with his friends. Each provides different rewards. That's normal. Finding ways to provide continuous proof of one's commitment to your significant other is important in building better relationships: "Is you is, or is you ain't my baby?!"

Google reported that in 2014 approximately 28% of couples in the US were living together out of wedlock (with 47% of children born out of such arrangements). Why? Two reasons: the adverse effect on income of married couples eligible for social welfare when one or both are unemployed, and, secondly, the unwillingness of human beings to commit to long-term relationships. Is it normal, for example, for some married men to be attracted to other women and to pretend that commitments are kinda temporary and that maybe there is someone better out there. Are they letting their more animal instincts override their human need for permanency, stability, and long-lasting mutually satisfying relationships? That need for connection is sometimes frightening, because it means cutting off the possibility of further experimentation and sexual exploration. It's not just men; sometimes women are also frightened of committing themselves to unknown long-term lives. Who knows what the future will bring in this committed relationship? That's why the divorce rate is so high; expectations go unfulfilled once the bloom is off the rose.

Before you can find fulfillment outside the relationship, you need to find fulfillment inside the relationship, on two levels: with yourself and with your partner. You can't commit to your partner until you can commit to yourself – to make yourself the best person you can be, to be comfortable in your own skin. And that means taking a realistic look at your qualities and faults and accepting that you are in the privileged position of being the one to deal with any shortcomings. Once you can accept yourself for who you are, you are able to accept the other person for who they are, warts and all. The sad fact is that some people never find satisfaction within themselves and are, as a result, unable to commit to another.

The power of the scepter

Relationships are about power, influence and control. The best relationships are about making sure both parties get what they want with the support of the other. Since neither party is certain of their needs or wants in the eternally shifting sands of time, flexibility is key. When do you push for your priorities and when do you become an advocate for theirs? What happens if you change your mind? In any relationship someone has to be the decision-maker. Can you both be joint decision-makers? Perhaps. But consider what happens if it all turns out pear-shaped. Who gets the blame? "It was your idea!" "I was just going along with you." You've probably been there. So when the time comes to make a joint decision, decide who has the scepter, and make it clear that they are making the decision alone.

Everyone needs to learn from the decisions they make. Therefore, the scepter of power should be in the hands of the person who has the strongest desire for the particular outcome at that time. After all, achieving an outcome is a natural motivator for human beings, just as long as it is the desired outcome of the person with the scepter and not the person of lower status at that time. The power in a relationship shifts according to who has the higher status and decides which outcome has the highest priority at that moment. That person becomes the decision-maker, the other becomes the supporter – and back and forth it goes. Relationships fail, however, when one person holds onto the scepter of power too long or begins to twirl it like a baton at the front of the parade. Power is best used with a more subtle grip, especially if you want to retain it and/or regain it over time.

There will be times when you have the scepter but the wise move is to give it away. This is actually what good leaders do much of the time: they set things up so that the people they are leading are able to achieve their goals by themselves – because the leader has been instrumental in creating the right conditions for that to happen. It's subtle, and it's powerful. Sometimes, in order to get what you want, in order to win you first have to lose. Let the other person get their way so that they feel satisfied and are, in turn, willing to let you have what you want.

This principle also applies in loving relationships. In order to be loved, you have to give love, and that may mean playing lower status, giving up your control, relinquishing the scepter of power. You want people to be attracted to you. You want people to love you, but you can never force that on others. You have to allow them the option to walk away, to let them leave you. Otherwise you are back in paradox country: "I want to you want me, but you have to really want to want me, not just because I want you to." And so on. Don't go there; it won't do your brain any good.

Regret

You never have all the information you'd like for making a decision. Information on its own is not enough. At some point you have to choose, based on some gut feeling or emotional response. You cannot be truly rational. One aspect of building trust is being decisive. If you are viewed as indecisive, people won't trust you. So, if you're ever stuck, making any decision is better than none. When you are faced with a high degree of uncertainty, do as the futurist Paul Saffo advocates: have "strong opinions weakly held" (Saffo, 2008). That means committing yourself to a particular course of action, finding out where it takes you and being willing to admit failure if it turns out not to get you where you want. Then you make another firm decision about what to do next and boldly go – which is far better than hanging back. People hesitate because they don't want to make a bad decision or they fear being wrong but there are no guarantees about what will happen. Your life has been a series of learning from your mistakes. So if and when the decision you do make is wrong, apologize and correct the mistake. People will forgive you and you will have built trust.

CHAPTER 29

Different Realities

T HIS BOOK IS A MIXTURE of secrets about how to have good relationships as well as how to avoid making things worse. There are always difficulties in every relationship because people think differently about their lives and about the world in general. Some of these differences make the other person interesting, whilst other divergent characteristics drive you nuts. So managing a relationship is about steering a course that sails more towards the former and away from the latter. Or it's about ways of changing your perceptions so that you find those difficulties are actually quite interesting. Saying, "I'm curious about why you do that. Tell me about it" makes a difference.

Perceptual Differences

To some extent, we conform to the stereotypes listed in Chapter 1: Drivers, Amiables, Analyticals and Creatives, and in a general sense we organize our experience in those kinds of ways. We want to know what things are and gather data; we want to know how to do things, how to get things to work; or we're interested in people and gossip and how to maintain our status. Or we wonder where all this information could possibly lead, how to develop this into something more interesting. That is to say, our different points of view will lead us to make sense of what is objectively the same information in the same context. We will each interpret it according to our life history, our preferences, habits and our current needs. So what you see as two people having a debate, others may interpret as a quest for dominance or just a continuation of a game that these two people are playing.

Not so long ago I was at a meeting, where there were the beginnings of a heated argument between two factions – one was all hi-tech and computer savvy and wanted information to arrive electronically on all kinds of modern devices; whilst the other was wanted communications to be made the old-fashioned way on bits of paper. These people wanted nothing to do with computers. Now, looking at this from a psychological point of view, I could see this as an example of 'learned helplessness'. Someone else might see this as the surfacing of some deep resentment coming from a past hurt. Others might see this as the democratic principle in action, or the need for some people to make a public show just to get noticed. It takes all sorts, as they say.

Given that we make sense of the world around us in our own unique way, it's not surprising that we are, to other eyes, missing a lot. Focus is good, but it has an opportunity cost: we miss everything in the background. Necessarily so, because our working brain has only limited capacity for paying attention to the world around us; there are many things we literally do not see. For instance, think of that now-famous example of the invisible gorilla (Chabris & Simons, 2010). The point of that study is that when we are concentrating on something, we exhibit something like tunnel vision. During that time, nothing else exists for us.

We fall into habits of perception, only noticing what's relevant to meeting our everyday needs, and ignoring everything else. It reminds me of my friend who used to work for Pillsbury in downtown Minneapolis. He lived in Mound, Minnesota, which is 27 miles west of downtown, and used to commute every day. One day he decided to quit Pillsbury and start his own company. To do this, he needed a physical location for his startup. He asked me if I knew of any offices for lease. I told him that I didn't, but I pointed out that the most important word in the English language was the word 'notice' because you can't interact with your environment unless and until you

notice what's going on around you. He called me up a day
later, absolutely flabbergasted. On his 27-mile drive home that
evening, he had noticed 22 *For Lease* signs on various buildings
that he had never seen before in all of his trips back and forth
to downtown. Once his needs changed, other things became
obvious to him, things that had been invisible to him before.
Now he was literally seeing a different world.

As our needs change we develop new habits. When, for
example, you think it's time to buy another car, you start
noticing all sorts of alternatives driving around you: different
makes, models, colors, shapes, sizes of vehicles on the road.
When you finally do purchase a car, you then tend to notice
all the other cars on the road which match your own. Why?
You need to feel some reassurance that you bought the right
car, and the fact that others made similar choices give you the
feeling that you made the correct decision. You also have an
unconscious need to belong to a group of people just like you.
You might even feel tempted during the first couple of weeks of
driving your new car to wave at people driving the same vehicle.
If so, please restrain yourself.

In any relationship, then, it would be worth exploring what you
are not seeing of your partner's or colleague's world. It's easy
to take them for granted and fail to notice that they are behaving
differently (you didn't expect them to change) or even their
physical appearance: "Didn't you used to have a beard?" That
might suggest that they won't notice the changes you are making
in your way of relating. Domestically, you have probably have
had your blanks pointed out: "Didn't you see ...?" "It was right
there in front of you, so how come you didn't notice it?" This
is in addition to losing your car keys and later realizing they
were right where you put them, in plain view. My wife calls this
'man eyes'. This is not only about vision, it applies to hearing as
well. "Did you hear what I said about ...?" Well, no you didn't
because you were too engrossed in watching sports on TV.

Problem? What problem?

The other person has a problem, and you're not sure why it's a problem. For you, it's not a problem; it's straightforward, you know what to do, because you've done things like that before, no big deal. But it's different for them; they can't see how easy it would be to ... And you don't understand why they can't see this.

One of the potential dangers in helping people solve problems is thinking that you understand what their problem is. Tidy minds make lists, organize data into patterns, perform statistical analysis, and so on. So for many human difficulties there exists a huge history and analysis of different types of problem. The internet is full of solutions written by people promoting their particular way of doing things. Pop in some key words and, Hey, problem solved! Well, perhaps if you want to know how to mend a broken chair, but not if you want to mend a broken relationship. Because then there is no guarantee that the information is correct or valid for your particular situation. This is something you can't really outsource; you have to do it yourself, step by step. And every step you take changes the situation to some degree, so you have to keep adjusting yourself.

This is why in the book I stress the importance of asking questions – mainly to clarify the situation, so that you know where the other person is coming from and where they are going: "How is this different now?" If you don't do this, you may just be making things worse.

Hooking

When you start trying to understand what the other person's problem is, you try to reduce your cognitive strain (aka not having a clue) by searching for the key that will open the door into their world. Because uncertainty can make us desperate to understand what's going on, we need to get a handle on the story someone else is telling by searching for the smallest clue. Until you get that, your mind will be frantically running possible scenarios in order to find one that works.

Quite often, the other person doesn't have a clear idea themselves, and so the first part of their talk is a confusing bunch of vague or half-finished statements that don't hang together. This makes you more eager to find the key that will open up the context for you. You're listening and waiting for a word – such as 'work', 'boss', 'school', 'in-laws', and so on – a clue that indicates which store of relevant stories you need to draw on and thus reduce the tension of not knowing.

The danger is that because of your training (in other words, the way you typically make sense of the world), you will hear a word or phrase that means something to you, and assume that's what the issue is about. This is called 'hooking'. Once you have caught your fish, you are going to serve it up with lemon and parsley, even if it's the wrong fish. You don't need to hear any more so you stop listening and start rehearsing in you mind what you would do. You're ready to launch your preferred one-size-fits-all solution.

With luck you will have selected the right cue. Even so, it's easy to run off in all directions and miss their reason for being there, because you both have different meanings for a common word or phrase. Worse still if they are using euphemisms or metaphors: "He's not happy at school" or "Our relationship is not firing on all cylinders." It's always worth checking out that you are in the same ballpark: "You mean your sex-life is unsatisfactory?" or "This is about bullying at your kid's school, isn't it?" – otherwise you will be wasting time talking at cross purposes.

A professional point of view could make things worse. For example, a couple in marital difficulties seek advice. Should they visit a legal person, the word that comes to mind is 'divorce'; if they visit a counselor, then obviously what they need is 'counseling'. An appointment with a mediation service means seeing the solution in those terms, and so on. The background training of the expert determines how they see the case, and limits the kind of solutions offered. Once they have hooked onto something the client has said, their whole armory is brought into play.

When this happens, it's possible that the two parties are talking at cross-purposes. The potential client is weaving their story of marital discord, or whatever, wondering how the marriage can be saved, yet the professional is actually organizing a timetable of divorce proceedings. This only compounds the problem, because you have two people talking past each other on different subjects. You have what's called *dual monologues*, which only leads to a new conflict developing. One solution is to call a halt, and point out that you are not being listened to. If the professional cannot adapt, then it's time to walk out.

Stereotyping the perceived problem so that it fits some standardized resolution is another danger. Stop. Don't do this. Something more is required – or rather, something less. Being a good listener may often be enough. The change comes as the other person manages to put their thoughts and feelings into words – and that's the beneficial part. All they need is the opportunity to do this with a sympathetic listener. No advice, no suggestions, no "why don't you's" are necessary. Indeed, they only interfere with the process of getting clear.

CHAPTER 30
Your Side Of the Relationship

"An S.E.P." he said, "is something that we can't
see, or don't see, or our brain doesn't let us
see, because we think that it's somebody else's
problem. That's what S.E.P. means. Somebody
else's problem. The brain just edits it out: It's like
a blind spot. If you look at it directly you won't
see it unless you know precisely what it is. Your
only hope is to catch it by surprise out of the
corner of your eye.
~ DOUGLAS ADAMS, *Life, the Universe and
Everything*

S O LET'S TAKE A LOOK at why people, in general, have
difficulty seeing eye to eye about the world around them
and how to fix some of the perceptual differences.

Eye to Eye
Human beings have a common way in which we collect
information in our environment, organize it in our minds, and
interpret this information. We select information based on our
expectations, needs and wants. People will live up to or down
to the expectations we have of them. If we don't expect much
from someone, that's exactly what we'll get – not much. If, on
the other hand, we have high expectations, we are more likely
to notice the other person's exceptionalism. You have to be
careful, however, that you don't set your expectations so high
that it becomes impossible for the other person to meet the
threshold criteria. If the expectations you place on someone else
are unrealistically high, especially if they have no idea of what
your criteria are, then you may be setting yourself up for a series

of disappointments leading to relational collapse. For example, in an angry outburst you accuse the other person of crossing the line, which may be news to them if you have never made explicit the limits to your personal value-system – or where exactly this line is to be found.

So, before you reach crisis point, how do you overcome these interpersonal differences? The focus is on you, not the other person. What matters is the way you respond to other people, because the ball's in your court. You need to change yourself. And that starts with you having a good relationship with yourself. Some people have this already; others are in the habit of beating themselves up for not living up to some fictitious high standards they have imposed.

Having spent some time together, you have probably drawn up a list of 'things my partner does that are not the way I do things' or something similar. Things that annoy you, irritate you, bewilder you. You may also notice a kind of negative bias here. So it's a good plan to widen your focus of attention, and discover the positive things your partner does as well: "Oh, she's really good at putting people at their ease" or "He has a great way of bringing humor to a situation." If you want the relationship to improve and develop, then focus on what each of you does that works. How do you respond to each other and the context you are in? Take a moment after some event or experience to notice what went well, and where you need to try a different tactic.

The Imitation Game: Fake it till you make it.

In my experience I find that most people often lie to themselves in order to feel better. We may not mean to lie – it's just that we frequently don't have any hard information on which to make a reasoned judgment, and we're actually quite lousy at making accurate judgments anyway, especially about ourselves. For a start, we estimate that we're above average at pretty much everything because we cherry-pick which information we base this judgment on. For example, we may think we're generous and charitable but don't give to charity. For me, our behaviors actually define our values, not the other way around. If I were truly charitable, I'd give. My sought-after values (like being charitable) are really goals, not reality. So if you want to change your actual values rather than live in a world of delusional ones, start by changing your behaviors. Gradually, your values start to align. In other words, you fake it till you make it. It's a way of overcoming cognitive dissonance – that's the internal pressure you feel when there is a difference between how you behave and what you believe.

In personal relationships, you may want to be closer to a potential spouse, so you look for ways to change your behaviors to be more compatible with them. But if your values don't then change, your behaviors eventually revert to your prior habits and the relationship falls apart. If you really want permanent change, you need to focus on consistently modifying your behaviors until they become habitual – and your actual values change. Don't try to change everything at once. That's not going to work because it will bring on too much cognitive strain. You need to concentrate on one particular change – preferably one that if you change that, it will have a knock-on effect on other behaviors. Changing something in your environment may help you do this – for example, hiding away or getting rid of items that you no longer want to consume or stopping doing things that your partner moans about because it annoys them. A good place to start is with these simple things. It's like the story of noticing things for the first time. Now that your attention has been drawn to them, remain aware of them and they will act as cues to remind you that it's time to do something different. It will take time and practice, and a period of constant behavioral monitoring to stay on track. Remember: Practice makes Permanent. After a while the changes in your behavior become the new normal and you find that your values have shifted to align with your behaviors.

The actor-observer bias

In trying to achieve closure, we run up against this particular bias in the way we explain things. The actor-observer bias is a social psychology term that refers to a tendency to attribute one's own actions to external causes, while attributing other people's behaviors to internal causes or character traits. Failure to be aware of this bias in attributing cause is likely to get in the way of understanding the situation. Essentially, people tend to make different attributions depending upon whether they are the actor or the observer in a situation. In everyday life, when something negative happens to you, you are more likely to blame it on chance, or the situation or circumstances. "Nothing to do with me; it was just bad luck." On the other hand, when you observe something negative about another person, it's far easier to believe that it was somehow built into them: it's their genes or their upbringing that resulted in them making poor choices, or engaging in undesirable behaviors. It fits in well with stereotyping.

Research has shown that you're less likely to apply this bias with people you know well, such as close friends and family members. In those cases, we have more empathy for those people and a lot more information about what drives them, how they think and so on. We acknowledge that they behave and react much like we do ourselves, and probably feel the same way about what happens.

"You started it"

Ever used this as an excuse for carrying on? It's common with children, but it doesn't really die out in adulthood. It comes from our need to create stories that explain our experience using cause and effect. It's another aspect of the actor-observer bias. Since the present situation must have had initial causation, then that must have been an external event (nothing to do with me), and the most likely suspect is whoever else was around at the time. Trouble is, this other person looks around and attributes the causation to you.

> "He started it!" is a common complaint, often heard on both sides, because each side attributes its own behavior to the situation but the others' behavior to their traits and other dispositions. It seems natural to infer that they are fighting because they are mean, whereas we are fighting because they attacked us. Or, in the simpler words of pro hockey play Barry Beck on a brawl that broke out in one game, 'We have only one person to blame, and that's each other!'"
> ~ BAUMEISTER & BUSHMAN, 2014:166

The way out of this impasse? One way is to forget about the history and focus on the outcome you desire. What do we want, and how are we going to achieve it?

MIRROR MIRROR • 185

Mirror Mirror

You Can't Please Everyone All The Time:
As hard as you try, you can't fix everybody – or anybody for that matter. You might think that the world would be a much better place if everyone saw the world the way you see it and acted accordingly. Too bad. That's not the way the world works; it thrives on variation and difference. That's what makes it an interesting place to live. Part of the challenge is learning to deal with difference, not about blasting it out of the water.

The hard part of building better relationships is to be able to get both people's needs met without conflicting with each other. In *Getting To Yes* (Fisher & Ury, 1981) the authors talk about four principles of negotiations, one of which was finding common interests. Most people go into a negotiating situation assuming that both parties naturally desire different outcomes, which implies there will be a need for a negotiation. If instead you assume there are some common interests and you start a negotiation looking at the interests of each of the parties, you may often find that they are not in conflict with each other, just different. It's not a zero-sum game where in order for one to win, the other has to lose. By looking at interests from the beginning, you may very well find yourselves on the same side of the table. Then you can work in concert to try to meet each other's interests so that both parties can get what they want.

Changing other people
I think it's worth repeating: Don't try to change the other person. It doesn't work, it wastes your time and simply reinforces their resistance to change. And let's face it, much of the time you

yourself will resist change.

Perhaps your partner or colleague is engaging in a behavior that is either not good for them – too much alcohol, or drug-abuse, or addictions of various kinds – and you spend your time trying to get them to change, or telling them to "Stop doing this." Such strategies are unlikely to work. Seldom does the other person say, "Oh, yes, thanks. You're right. I'll stop that immediately." Doesn't happen. They have developed sophisticated ways of brushing off outside comments on their behavior – they are just brilliant at justifying what they do or superb at convincing themselves that it's really OK to do whatever and that you are just worrying about nothing. "Sure, I could give this up. But it gives me pleasure." Or there is some other need that is being met – which neither you nor they may be consciously aware of. So until you find another way to meet that need, nothing's going to change.

What to do instead? One passive solution is to be a role model for them. Act as you would wish others to behave: be tidy, communicate clearly, and so on, and hope – and hope is necessary because you're not going to ram anything down their throats – that they will find you inspiring and wish to copy you.

They may choose not to. Or they may be so wrapped up in their own worlds that they just don't notice. Are people happy living with their problems, lousy relationships, difficult colleagues and partners? Sometimes, yes. They get used to it … until the moment arises when they snap! By which time it may be a little late for sorting things out; instead, it's goodbye. (More on that in Chapter 40.)

Get to know yourself

An essential aspect of getting along with someone else is that you first need to get along with yourself. Take a good long look in the mirror and figure out what it is you like about yourself and what you don't. What it is that you want to be, to do, to improve, to accomplish. Many people do things that they think will make others happy. In the process, they lose themselves because they have forgotten their own needs. As I said right at the beginning, happiness is not a rational goal. And it's especially true that you cannot make someone else happy and fulfilled; their happiness has to come from within them. They may even get unhappy because they see you're so happy!

So, time to be a bit selfish and figure out what it is you want in life. Problem is, that's hard. It's hard because you have a whole bunch of conflicting thoughts jumbled up in your head – the *oughts* and *shoulds* – making it a real challenge to sort out what it is you truly want. People make demands, they keep pushing and pulling you in different directions and you seem to be running as fast as you can but getting nowhere and pleasing no one.

Blind Spots

It's easy for some people to drift through life on automatic. It saves a lot of thinking, living in a dream, not connecting, not joining the dots. Your days are mapped out: it's fish on Fridays and holidays in Florida in the RV. Why worry? Well, maybe you're missing out on having a richer and fulfilling life.

Take a moment to consider how much you might be missing. Do you get any kind of feeling that something's missing in your life? How long have you been coasting through life? And is that how you want the rest of your life to be? Should you book your place in the retirement home now to avoid disappointment later?

Think about your life right now. How does this connect with your youth, and your youthful ideals (or had you given up even then?). Did you ever think "I want to do X" or "Wouldn't it be great to achieve Y"? What happened to those dreams? Did they get put on hold, and then put in sleep mode?

Perhaps, for whatever reason, 'Me time' has been banished: "I have to look after … the kids, my aging parents, my spouse, my team …" There is never a shortage of excuses, and when you bring one up into your awareness, it kind of blocks out any good idea that you could apply to yourself. What would it be like to think "I have to look after me." What would that involve? Check out your feelings first – any guilt, fear, confusion? Would it be selfish? What would others think of you? Actually, it's very likely that they would admire you, and wish they could do the same.

It's not just about pampering, though that could be a good idea once in a while. It's more about long-term care – not the sort you'll get in that retirement home, but in the here and now, improving your way of being in the world. How fit are you? How flexible? How do you flow through life? Is it a series of lurches, lumberings, backtrackings. Or have you learned to roll with the swell of the tides and the roughness of the terrain? What would help you do that? You no doubt know the answers to those questions because you have survived thus far.

So take some time, without distractions, to think about the things you would like in your life. Some will be wishes that would be tough to fulfill. But that's not the point. You are thinking about how your life could be richer, more exciting, more satisfying. It's now too late for the 'if only's' – because it always is. Take up yoga, pilates, tai chi, mindfulness, meditation … the list is endless, and probably overwhelming. How do you choose? Would any of them do you some good? You'll never know until you try. How much of a disruption to your life would that entail? So what if that time you've now recovered from useless worry about others, you were to use to benefit yourself. Would that make you happier?

Be Spontaneous

Although you can't force others into acting spontaneously, you can act as a role model. So trust the situation and actually be spontaneous yourself. Learning to act on impulse, improvising, doing things in the moment takes practice – often it's something you need to give yourself permission to do. So respond to impulses, spend more time in the moment. As long as you're not putting yourself in danger or harming other people, what is there to lose? Go for that walk, paint the bedroom, write to that friend you haven't seen for a while. It's more about saying Yes to an idea, to suggestions put by someone else, especially if it's an activity you have never done before, something that would break up your routine or take you out of your comfort zone. The other person thinks whatever they do is worthwhile, so if you join them you might find yourself enjoying it too. And you are building your relationship with them. They are also giving you a way of expanding your awareness, so that you'll begin to notice what you do not normally notice. Like my friend looking for office space to lease, you'll change what you pay attention to and notice more of what's actually going on. Ask, "What am I not seeing?" or "What else is there?"

Time together

Hang around someone who is an expert in their job or hobby, and you'll begin to notice the fine distinctions they make in what they do – the quality of the light at different times of the day, the subtleties of harmony in musical compositions. At the same time, you'll be learning about their life, how they see the world, what it's like to be them.

How much time do you actually spend with the significant others in your life? Do a quick, honest survey. Jot down a list of names: spouse, children, work team … and then estimate how much time you spent with each individual during the last week. No good saying, "Last week was exceptional"; your aim is to make every week exceptional – for those you care about. Do you need to make any adjustments here? Perhaps adding more time for just chilling out together, rather than planning specific activities.

If the situation could be improved, then ask yourself: What is it in my lifestyle that gives rise to this pattern? What is driving me to behave like this? Because to some extent, you have chosen to use your time in this particular way. Sure, there are the constraints of working and commuting – but these are not set in stone. How do you fill your 'free' time? Do you try to be busy every moment? If so, why? Where does that belief or attitude come from? Is there something wrong about doing nothing or not very much? It's a common belief that you should be constantly productive, and it's often a belief that affects your children's lives. You see the world as competitive and that in order to win you have to spend every moment doing useful things that will help you achieve. But this can be a very stressful way of living. The good news is you can do something about it. Look at your list of activities and decide what your priorities are. What really matters? What is there of marginal interest that could be dropped? There is an opportunity cost here. You can't do everything, but what you do do prevents you from doing something else. There's always a trade-off. Ask yourself: If I were to stop doing X, who would care, who would suffer? How could I get more benefit from the limited time I have available?

Reducing clutter

Not just physical clutter – which is always worth getting rid of – but mental clutter as well. Some of your beliefs and attitudes you may have been carrying with you since childhood – and they may be way past their best-before date. This is about habits of mind, where you are focusing your attention. Have you adopted a WIIFM (what's in it for me?) attitude, just looking after your own interests, or do you want the best for other people? If you are constantly concerned or worried about what other people might be thinking of you, this is also raising a barrier that stops you being fully present for them. Some dearly held beliefs, such as thinking you have solutions to other people's problems, may need to go out in the trash.

Whenever you hit a problem, or find yourself responding strongly to some event mentioned in the newspaper or on TV, or find people arguing with you, instead of digging your heels in, consider that this could be a moment of change and liberation – if you allow yourself to consider the alternatives. Think through what you believe: "Is this really the case? Is this supported by evidence?" and decide whether it's time to update. Same applies to challenging any behaviors that are stopping you being fully who you could become.

CHAPTER 32
Martial Arts Vs. Marital Arts

THE IMPERFECT LIFE
For most people, their behaviors are determined by their core values and beliefs. These values and beliefs are built up from birth with the influence of family, friends, teachers, the community, and so on. From about age five on, they are pretty much set in stone, unless some significant emotional event comes along to shake up their belief system. As we mature, we naturally run across challenges to these beliefs from other, perhaps conflicting, views that test this bond. But, because our values are so deeply seated ... part of our unconscious self, they are nearly impossible to change. Our behaviors are an outward symbol of our inner beliefs and are, therefore, equally difficult to change. Our behaviors are habitual. And we all know how hard it is to break or change our habits. Anyone tried to lose weight lately? Or make New Year resolutions? We're on autopilot for most of our lives.

Now, here you are, with this other person, each complete with habits built up over a lifetime, wanting to make this relationship work. No two people are identical; they have habits they've grown accustomed to, which they really resist changing. In order to become compatible with this other person, we make adjustments. Some adjustments are easy and no big deal: who takes the first shower, who makes the coffee, who makes the presentation to the boss this time, who takes the notes in the next meeting, who leads, who follows, who talks, who listens. Easy. Other adjustments, however, are more difficult, because you need to know exactly what the difference is. This is why I have listed some key factors below, so that you can begin to see what was not apparent before.

For some individuals, going along to get along can initially be very difficult, but gradually it tends to get easier. It's like stretching a rubber band: keep stretching it and the tension lessens over time. Just don't stretch it until it breaks. Everyone has a breaking point in terms of compromising with the needs of others. Find out what adjustments others are willing or able to accommodate or not and what you are willing to compromise or not, and for what length of time. This helps relationships grow and last.

You might think that in adapting to the other person you are just being weak. Are you simply avoiding confronting them about some problem? It depends how far this goes. If the other person believes that their way is right and that you will continue to adjust to them, then this is an unbalanced relationship that could lead on your part to frustration and more. There needs to be some understanding of difference and a movement on their part towards making mutually acceptable adjustments. One possibility is to ask them to make explicit their rules, values, and so on. They may have never done this before, and it may surprise them. Once these are in the open, they may realize that some of them are out-of-date (they were only useful when they were a child), overly restrictive (there may have been a security scare at one time, but this is no longer a threat), or just plain bizarre. Then it becomes obvious to them that they need to update. However, if beliefs are deeply held, they are part of you, and there's probably not much going to change in the near future.

What you are up against is the fact that people don't like to admit that they want to change or get better. Sometimes they need permission – not just from you or other people, but from themselves. So you have to make it ok for them to do this. It may be a good idea to elicit the criteria for change: "So what would need to happen for you to do this?"

It might be worth going down the path of asking: "Has this

always been true?" Chances are that a belief was adopted at a certain time; before that it was not part of their system. "So what changed?" Could you perform a computer-style System Restore on your belief system?

Can you spot the storm coming? Have you 'been here before'? If you do recognize the signs, then practice doing something different. You have to take the lead. If you expect the other person to change spontaneously you could be in for a long wait. And you're certainly not going to play the childish game of You Have to Change First – the bugbear of many a negotiation that goes nowhere.

You could be upfront and say "We've been in this position before. And we know it doesn't work. So what could we do instead?"

Consider third-party results: "Who do we know who has solved this problem?" "Who managed to get out of such an impasse?" This is where the internet comes in handy. There's a good chance that something sensible has been written about it somewhere. Your job is to sort the wheat from the chaff and find something that you can adapt and use yourselves.

That is also a good diversionary tactic. You're switching the focus of attention away from the gap between you to a space out there in the neutral territory where you are both explorers together. The trick comes in knowing how to assess the advice you find. There is the danger that you only seek information that supports your position – the so-called 'confirmation bias' – and that only polarizes the situation further.

This is about taking the pressure off in the moment. Anything that does this will be useful. It's about cooling off, calming down, avoiding a direct confrontation.

For example, metaphorically, you might imagine you're using a

Selfie Stick to take a picture of the current situation. What does it look like from that distance? What does the camera see of both of you together? Any technique that gets you to step back, gain some perspective, is going to be useful here. One traditional device is called playing Devil's Advocate. That is, you take on a different role by saying, "Let me play Devil's Advocate for a moment" and you then give an objective account of what's going on, arguing against the position you prefer to take. You're looking at the downside and the consequences of taking action and of doing nothing. There is of course the danger that you come across as a know-it-all, and the other person slips into the role of shooting the messenger – but that's life. For example,

- "What would X say about this?" where X is a respected relative, friend, public figure.
- Speak in the third person: "What if Mary were to step back for a moment …"
- Take on a fly-on-the-wall perspective and tell it like it is from there.
- Talk in quotes "If I were to say that, how would you react?" (You're still saying what you want to say but adding a barrier layer, holding the statement at arm's length, so to speak.)

Get them thinking about the situation, engaging with you in a joint enterprise to solve the problem. Say, for example, "So how does it appear to you?" "What's your take on this?" The aim is to get a relevant response from the other person, and to avoid anger, abuse, put-downs, or clamming up.

What you want is for the other person to take the *process* seriously. Therefore, it has to be safe for them to talk about things they may never have made public before. That means allowing the silence. Once you have asked the question, shut up. Wait. It may seem like ages, and you're bursting to intervene with a follow-up question or make hurry-up expressions. But don't. Stay neutral. And whatever you do,

- Don't make jokes.
- Don't tease, use sarcasm, irony.
- Don't talk down or use putdowns
- Don't bring up past misdemeanors.
- Don't interpret for them.
- Thank them for their input.

Battle-based relationships versus bendable-based relationships

Franky and Johnny met at a fraternity party. People enjoyed Franky, up to a point. When challenged, she became loud and defensive. I'm not sure that alcohol didn't add to the tension. People would back away from her when she was irritated. Except for Johnny. He would volley back her best shots. Franky enjoyed being with Johnny because he wasn't intimidated by her. They fell in love and eventually married. Over the years they would fight with each other over petty things. Things that didn't really matter. They were in a continually battling pattern. After a while, they grew tired of the constant battles and sought couples counseling. Why? Because their relationship had been based on challenging each other; battling, after all, showed strength, right? Neither one want to appear weaker in the eyes of the other. But over time they changed; they wanted a closer and deeper relationship.

"Why do we have to fight every time we make a decision?"

Neither was willing to give in as they thought that showing weakness to the other meant they would lose their respect. Because their initial attraction was based on the battle, changing that unspoken agreement might doom their relationship. So now it was time to find a new basis for their relationship, one that was going to see them through the next phase of their life together. But if no common ground could be found, they would need to consider whether staying together was a viable option.

Control issues

Some people want to know that they can control the other person. Not that they would do this all the time, but that they could if they wanted to. Sometimes control is one partner's response to the other's uncertainty or lack of expertise. This happens in business a lot. A newly promoted manager tries to micro-manage the replacement simply because they know the job. But what they are doing is denying the new subordinate the opportunity to learn, to make mistakes or to find their own ways of achieving desired outcomes.

Some forms of martial arts are about control and domination, about battling to win. The aim is to achieve control, but first you have to bend to the will of the opponent. That's the way to gain in the end. Aikido, for example, uses the force of the other against them: at first bending, giving in, and then utilizing the energy the opponent is expending to direct them into their own downfall. In that way, they lose control and you gain it. Some people have a need to be right all the time. You may find that by letting them win they loosen up and give you what you want in return. They just needed to feel that win under their belt to gain self-gratification. Once the win is achieved they become more accommodating.

Not My Pig, Not My Farm

So you've reached an impasse. You're face to face with the enemy. Now you need to decide whether to engage with them. This is a matter of thinking through the consequences and deciding if the hassle is worth it. Some battles are worth fighting, but they will take their toll, in terms of reputation, time and effort. So it's important to pick your battles with those people with whom you would like to either build or maintain a positive relationship.

Forego the battle – because the momentary satisfaction of winning is not what it's about – and go for support instead. How much are you willing to risk losing by winning at all costs?

The whole point of the pig/farm analogy is that you need to pick your fights ... especially if you get the feeling that your opinion might cause tension between the primary players in the discussion. Is it worth it to say what's on your mind or is it best to keep your opinions to yourself. My wife introduced this saying to me as well as the phrase "Quick! Check your face. I found a nose in my business!"

Always respect others. Be polite – even if you don't like them. They'll possibly pick up the leakage in your body-language, but no matter, they're probably used to that, and that's not going to be the key issue at stake. Don't use sarcasm, putdowns, and especially do not show contempt. Contempt is one of the surefire ways of recognizing that a relationship is on the rocks and about to founder.

The Marital arts focus on winning together, helping the other win, especially if the result is important to your partner. The result may not necessarily be important to you. It's very rare indeed for two people in a successful relationship to have created a zero-sum game in which for me to get what I want, I have to make sure that you lose. Marital arts is about finding common goals that you can fight for together while simultaneously supporting each other's individual goals. So she gets to plant flowers in the garden, and he gets the vegetables, but hey, they're both getting the pleasure of gardening – it's a win–win.

It's never a good idea to tell negative stories about the other person in public. Although it may seem to be a funny story to you, it's not your place to downgrade them in front of strangers, and it doesn't show either of you or your relationship in a good light. So however tempting it is, hold your tongue. Instead, give people support in public – they are members of your family or team, and they deserve public recognition. This is about knowing where and when to keep quiet. It's a form of gossip otherwise, and essentially, what happened is irrelevant. Think: what did I learn from that? That's for you to know.

Banging on the Bus: Co-dependency

A while back, my wife and I went on a vacation to the Dominican Republic. We felt the need to just get away from the frozen north for a few days, lie in the tropical sun and relax.

On one of the days we decided to go on a day trip to a place called Paradise Island. Paradise Island is nothing like it sounds. It took a two-hour bus ride to the dock/beach where our hardy troop of fellow travelers flopped into a motorized row boat taking us about 100 yards to our catamaran/floating bar. Let the drinking begin. An hour or so later, we arrived at our destination; a spit of sand about 30 yards long and 30 feet wide surrounded by tour boats and inhabited by five small shacks chaotically distributing masks and flippers to half-drunk yelling Germans. Flippers were flying; masks grabbed, it was all great fun. Think Department Store during their annual sale. As we snorkeled, there was even a floating bar just to make sure we didn't notice the chaos and flailing snorkelers. The few sober Germans sat in the shade of one of the shacks, talking and shaking their heads. "Stupid Americans."

While the snorkeling was decent (great reefs), we were all happy to be back on board and heading to shore to catch our bus for the two-hour return trip to the resort. As we all belly flopped off the side of the row boat onto the beach, we were hot, tired, and anxious to get on the bus. Unfortunately, we were not allowed on the bus until our tour guide gave the OK, which was only after everyone had a chance to buy something in the gift shop (think Disney model). That's when it happened.

The few of us bypassing the buying opportunity and waiting patiently in the heat and humidity for the bus to pull up from the parking lot noticed a solo figure making her way slowly to the bus, a bit on the unsteady side. It was Barbara. Barbara had been drinking from the minute we arrived on the catamaran until we dinghyed to shore. And why not? It's all included. She didn't bother with flippers, preferring instead to find comfort attached to the floating bar.

But there she was. We all looked on in stunned amazement when she approached the closed door to the bus, raised her fists above her head and started pounding on the glass; screaming at the top of her lungs, "Let me in, dammit!!" It was all kinda funny in a raging great ape sorta way. The tour guide was running towards her at full stride yelling something in Spanish. The Germans were yelling what I assumed were curses in German. Even the sleeping dog raised his head nonchalantly to see what the ruckus was all about.

Standing behind Barbara was Todd, her husband, trying to calm her down. He was repeatedly mouthing "I'm sorry … I'm so sorry" to the few of us amused/stunned by the tirade. Once Todd had managed to coax Barbara onto the bus, the rest of us climbed aboard, and we all headed back to the hotel. Half-way there, we stopped at a famous cigar factory/shop to learn about the fine art of making and consuming carcinogens. Bypassing the shop again, my wife and I headed back to the bus ahead of the crowd. That's when I realized what true love was in the world of co-dependency. There already on the bus were Barbara and Todd. In a switch of roles, Todd was now being loud and obnoxious. The alcohol had finally reached his brain. Barbara was calming him down and making frequent trips into the shop to buy treats for Todd. It appeared to me that their relationship (an obviously loving one based on how they interacted with each other) was based on the need for each partner to take care of and protect the other, to make sure neither would be disgraced in public. In your relationship, what do you do when you're partner starts banging on the bus? Do you join them, criticize them, yell at them, or protect their dignity and self-worth? I just hope Todd and Barbara are never drunk at the same time.

CHAPTER 33

Fair Fighting

C OUPLES WHO STAY WITH EACH other need to find ways of handling the inevitable conflicts in caring positive ways, in which each supports the other person in what is for them a difficult time.

Problems can be put on the back burner, but it's unlikely they will go away completely. A better idea is to find time to deal with them. Now, given your everyday life, you're always in the middle of something – and don't want to be interrupted. And surprise, your partner is also in the middle of something and doesn't want to be disturbed. So what do you do? You make an appointment. Yes, arrange a time, later, when your busyness has finished, and you have time for each other. Don't plan too far ahead – just enough time to get your thoughts together, and the other essentials of living out of the way. It's probably best to choose neutral territory – not the bedroom, for instance. The kitchen is probably more multi-purpose – and there's a rack of knives handy ... Kidding! Going for a walk together is also a good way of moving things along.

When you become aware of some issue, and it's something that isn't going to go away without you doing something about it, then during the day find a brief moment to make an appointment for later, when you will talk about the issue together. Tell your partner what the topic is to be in sufficient detail so that they know what to think about, but don't offer solutions. For example: "These friends of mine are coming next week and they have two small children, so we need to think about how that's going to work here" or "I've noticed that you are not chatting with me in the way you used to, so I'm wondering if there is something you're not telling me." This is not about blaming the other person.

If you want to sort out an issue, then you need to be physically together in the same place and focused on the issue. This is probably not going to happen spontaneously – you need to plan this. One benefit of arranging something for later is that it gives you time to cool down and to think carefully about what you want to say and what you want to achieve. If you can't calm down in this time, then what's stopping you? What do you need to get out of the way? Are you running a mental dialogue with yourself over and over? If something else is going on for you, then perhaps you need to deal with that first. If it's an internal dialogue plaguing you, then imagine it's a recording and speed it up to get squeaky voices or run it backwards.

In the time before you actually get together to sort things out, consider: "What's really at stake here? I've had time to think about it, so is it about me, or is it about my partner? Or is it something outside of our relationship? How important is it?" You could even consider "In a hundred years' time how important would it be?" – that kind of puts it in perspective.

Set a time for your get-together. And remember to turn up. No excuses. Switch off the TV, turn off all possible distractions; you are not going to answer your phone. Remember, don't sit facing each other, because that suggests conflict. Sit side by side, or at an angle. The third corner of the triangle then becomes neutral space in which things will get sorted.

Even though it may feel artificial or embarrassing the first time, ignore these feelings because you have work to do. Be open, be honest, be humble. Don't make jokes or treat things lightly. Allow silences. But don't treat this as a board meeting. State how it seems from your point of view, without mind-reading your partner or assuming you know how they feel about things or how they will respond. Remember, good relationships maintain an element of surprise – even after years together.

When asked how they managed to stay married for over 40 years, Ben and Jenny said,

> "It wasn't easy, that's for sure. We nearly got divorced several times over the years. We even took a break from each other for a while to let things settle down." When I asked Ben why they didn't just call it quits, he said, "'cause I love her … and I think she loves me … or at least she tolerates me."

People fall into a pattern of comfort: the hurdles are known and can be coped with. They have a shared history that they don't want to lose … even if the relationship is based on throwing knives at each other.

Decide who goes first. Who is the 'problem owner'? State the problem. Stick to facts:

- The context: where and when. Is it a one-off, or does it frequently happen like this? When does it not happen?
- The event: X happens. What is the trigger? For example, when visitors are expected, when you get home from work.
- The consequences: As a result, Y also happens. Is any direct causal connection discernible here?
- How you respond to that, how you feel about it. "And it makes me feel …"
- What you would rather have happen?

Give the other person time to think about these things. They probably need a quiet moment to mull over what you have said, so don't interrupt, prompt or repeat things unless they ask you or want clarification.

Listen to each other. You may not like what you hear but you need to hear it. Although it might be difficult, resist becoming defensive. Remember this is just their perception of the matter, and, just like you, your partner will have their own prejudices and biases. Listen between the lines – and you may encounter some hard truths. You can't always be sure what you are hearing – we have inbuilt protective mechanisms that shield us from unpleasantness – so you need to ask for a repeat, or get your partner to clarify. Check that you are getting the important message, the thing that really bugs them. Saying "Let me see if I've got this right ..." adds a buffer and gives you time to think. It signals to the other person that you are not going to take what they said lying down. "So you are saying that ..." This is the first step. However, clarity on its own is not sufficient. You need to know what to do differently in future, you must think in practical terms: "So what's one thing I could do to improve or make it better?" It's a low-status approach. You want their understanding and expertise to guide you. It puts the ball back in their court.

In this way, you are spending time working together, caring about getting the relationship back on track. When you have discovered some ways forward, show your appreciation and love.

Look for solutions:
- Where would be the best place to intervene? Environment, Definition of terms, Ways of doing things, Priorities and values, Desired outcomes?
- Is it within your or the other person's power to change what needs to be changed?
If not, what would be the best alternative solution?
- Get agreement about the proposed solution, who will do what.
- Setting a time-frame is useful, and also set a date for a progress review.

Clarify what each person is expected to do in order to change things. Make it explicit: When, where, what, and with whom.

If it is not within someone's power to do what's needed, find out what they will be able to do instead. Is there a compromise solution available?

If the solution involves some kind of skill or particular way of saying things, have a practice session right there and then. (See Chapter 15 on feedback). Avoid the "I'll think about it" ploy; just have a go. It may seem strange at first – it's new, of course it feels peculiar – but it will become the new normal once you start using it.

Choose a reasonable length of time – not too short, not too long or you'll forget – to check in on the new way of doing things. Has the situation changed? Is the new way working? If not, then arrange another discussion to find a better solution.

CHAPTER 34
Dealing with Your Own Anger

WHAT IS THE POINT OF anger? We get angry when our expectations are thwarted. For whatever reason, someone else has behaved in such a way that our 'oughts' and 'shoulds' have been undermined. If it's just a clash of ideas, and we don't feel deeply and emotionally concerned, we are more likely to laugh. But when something personal and vital to the relationship has been violated then our feelings run high.

You feel justified in expressing anger because your partner or your team-mate has done something that could undermine the relationship, such as breaking trust, failing to honor a promise, cheating on you, lying to you or insulting you in front of other people. What's beneath the anger is fear: fear of loss, separation, rejection. It's more acceptable to express anger than to express hurt or vulnerability. So the anger becomes a form of defense – because you don't want to be rejected.

Anger is never about the other person. It's about how your expectations about the situation are not being met. It's cognitive dissonance again, our inability to hold conflicting beliefs simultaneously. People tend to get angry when surprised. People really don't like surprises since they have to react too quickly without having a chance to think things through, especially certain personality types, like Analyticals.

Although there is a long traditional belief that venting your anger is a good idea, the evidence now suggests that it is not (Tavris & Aronson, 2007). The ancient Greek idea of *catharsis* was adopted by Freudian psycho-analysis and has since enjoyed great popularity. The metaphor employed is treating emotions such as anger as some kind of fluid. It becomes something you bottle up. You can keep the lid on, but if the pressure builds up you can let it all out, or discharge it, although in the process you might become drained.

The cathartic notion was seen as a way of relieving the pressure, and a good way to do that was to shout and scream and hit things. This is certainly the image projected in a number of Hollywood movies (such as *The War of the Roses*), in which a character will go on a rampage and smash everything in sight. This is nothing more than the grown-up version of the temper tantrum which you might expect from a young child.

It has long been assumed that taking your anger out on some inanimate object – such as laying in to a punching bag, whacking a dummy with a baseball bat, or beating up a cushion or doll – is cathartic, that it discharges the emotional energy, and you'll feel better afterwards. For example, a factory in Japan was famous for having a "stress release" room. In this room was a 200+ pound sand-filled dummy hanging from the ceiling. Around the room were masks of all the factory supervisors (and blanks that you could draw on). When you needed a stress break, you would go into this room, close the door behind you, place your mask of choice onto the dummy, take one of the assorted stick swords from the wall, and spend the next few minutes beating the crap out of the dummy, until you were exhausted and drained of your stress. That probably says more about working in Japan than it does about best practice, because the truth is rather different.

What's more likely is that by venting your anger you feel you're justifying it. Instead of disappearing, your anger builds, your blood pressure increases, and your negative thoughts multiply. Your cathartic action justifies and reinforces your anger, so that next time a similar situation arises, you become more aggressive as a result. Some people report that having expressed anger in a loud and gesticulating way they then feel down and somewhat depressed afterwards and this may even last a few days.

However, this is not to say that you should never let off steam or release the tension. See this as a momentary thing, not as a prolonged attack. If you are angry, the anger should be recognized and released in some form – anything from a sharp release of breath (with or without some swearing) to banging your head against the wall. But that's it. No need to go on doing this. And whatever you do, do it in private, not in front of other people (they won't be impressed by your performance). You are not going to have any positive effect on the other person if you start shouting and screaming and jumping up and down. Making threats or insulting their genetic inheritance is a good way of lowering your status!

Lighten up the process by using pretend weapons. There is an ancient tradition in circus and silent movies of using custard pies. They're both serious and a joke at the same time, which is the point. Anger is an exaggerated form of humor, which is when two contradictory things happen at the same time. Often, we just laugh. But there are times when this is serious – you're being accused of some misdemeanor by someone you love, and you forget the funny side of it in the moment and get angry instead. But it's the same principle – we find it hard to entertain two versions of reality at once.

When I had my own private clinical practice I used to use a tool called 'encounter bats'. Couples would come to one of my sessions, talk a bit, then get their frustrations out by using these heavily foamed bats to hit each other harmlessly to get out their aggression and frustrations. Once tired, and usually laughing at that point, they would be able to better talk through their issues with each other.

Whether or not cathartic action is appropriate depends on you. The art is getting through the red mist to the belly laugh

– can you see the funny side? No? Then just imagine you are watching yourself being angry on a video. Aren't you just a little ridiculous, overdoing it? This is why the usual recommendation given in all those books and videos is: Count to ten (other numbers are available). Take time out. Breathe. Especially that. Deep breath. Because when you get angry you stop breathing. In the long term, that's not a good strategy.

Lose/Lose situations

> Gavin: There is no winning! Only degrees of losing!
> ~ DANNY DEVITO (1989) *The War of the Roses*

Let's return to the idea of relative status, and treat anger as lowering someone else's status.

- When someone directs anger at you, they are putting themselves as high status and putting you down. They are indicating that they know best and that their system rules.
- At the same time, you feel "I'm being ignored, trampled on, and I don't like it. You don't care about me. You think I'm worthless" and so on. Not a good position to be in.

So to build yourself up again you get angry or even angrier than they are – just to regain your position. But this is a fight that goes nowhere. No one can win. You have to stop playing the game.

Mind you, if the relationship itself has lost its status and you've got to the eye-rolling stage (Parker-Pope, 2002) then there's little chance of resurrecting it.

People who are comfortable in their own skin, who acknowledge their own strengths and flaws, may tend to get disappointed rather than angry: "It would have been better if ...", but realize that they do not wear a crown or have a magic wand.

They realize that showing anger may make them feel better momentarily but serves no greater purpose. We might rationalize the energetic aspect of anger as a warning display to the other person: "You have hurt me, diminished me, disrespected me in some way, and I want you to change your behavior." That's the intended message. Sometimes it might get through, and with luck they'll avoid doing things that annoy you. What's more likely is that they are temporarily blinded by their own need to be right. For example, when someone cuts you up on the highway, or queue jumps, their response will either be indifference – they know what they're doing and they're going to get their way regardless, and annoying you is an added bonus; or they will start to justify their actions to avoid cognitive dissonance – "I deserve this because …" We are never at a loss for finding justification. It's been found that if people offer any kind of reason for their behavior – "I need to be at the front of the queue because I'm in a hurry" or any feeble excuse, we tend to accept this.

There are also times when anger is ineffective or counter-productive. You're fired up with anger, and you want to do something to remedy the situation, but there is nowhere to direct your action: you are up against faceless bureaucrats or implacable forces of law and order … you know you are not going to get anywhere, and by kicking up a fuss, kicking the cat or the technology you may make it worse (and get arrested). Then you definitely need time to plan your next move, away from the situation.

Ways of dealing with anger

If it's the other person who is really angry, then how do you usually respond? Come on, you've had lots of practice, and you've found out what doesn't work. Retaliation might seem a good idea, but the long-term consequences would not support it. Revenge is only effective in destroying relationships (*The War of the Roses* again), and tends to lead to escalation: they will do it back to you only more so.

OK, someone has let fly at you. You've overcome your initial shock, and you are once more able to speak. Be careful what you say. If you go with, "What were you thinking of?" "What were you trying to achieve by doing this?", it might seem to be a rational response, but it's hard to say it without the undercurrent of blame and put-down. And the other person is probably not in the right state to give thoughtful answers.

Use non-defense

> "Up to a point, Lord Copper."
> ~ EVELYN WAUGH (1938) *Scoop*

You're going to lower your status voluntarily. You could think of this as submission but that's only the surface appearance. You are retaining your integrity. The attacker, the angry person, needs a target. But that's what you are not going to offer them. Adopt a martial arts approach. One way to avoid someone's anger is to not be there! However, if you do happen to be there, then it's time to leave; whatever's bugging them, that is something they need to sort out on their own, and you need to avoid doing anything to make the situation worse.

Failing that, refuse to be a target of someone else's anger. If you see anger as more about the person themselves, not about you, then anything coming your way needs to be deflected or absorbed harmlessly. Sounds easy, but it needs practice. You could turn into a block of stone so that the other person's slings and arrows bounce off you. Or you could go all wibbly-wobbly so that you are lacking any substance and things go straight through you. If you were to imagine they're firing bullets at you, then the sensible thing to do would be to move to one side so that you are not in the direct line of fire.

What could you do differently?

- Essentially you want to introduce something unexpected so that you break the pattern. Surprise the other person and they will respond differently. Then you have a better chance of sorting something out.
- While they are ranting, stay in neutral. Be that faceless functionary who's not going to have any cracks in the way they present themselves. So don't respond, however much your instincts tell you to.
- If the angry person is trying to belittle you by making general accusations: You always do X; you never do Y, then it's easy to go along with the vague idea. Use vague agreement as a form of pacification: "You could be right." "You may have a point."
- If they are beginning to calm down, acknowledge their state: "I can see you're angry. This must be difficult for you." And then direct their attention to what needs to happen: "Help me understand why. Explain what you want to happen differently."

If you know you have violated their norms or expectations, then apologize. Just say, "I'm sorry." Don't try to justify, explain or offer excuses. An apology should defuse their anger; they have won. When they are able to talk about what happened, you could say what you were trying to do, what your expectations were. You want to know what went wrong: "Please give me some feedback here. I want to know what to do so that I don't screw up next time."

If you consider that their anger is their stuff and nothing to do with you, then, used with caution, you could try these strategies:

- Refuse to be put down (Johnstone, 1981:51–2). The angry person expects to do you down, but instead you rise up. "Why did you read my emails?" reply "I always read your emails." "Why?" "I want to know what's going on." Treating such claims in a matter-of-fact way surprises them. This kind of response is unexpected, and deflects them from their plan of crushing you. Now they have to respond differently.

- Be curious – see their behavior as worthy of investigation and make a mental jump outside of the arena: "Do you always behave like this?" "That's interesting. Tell me more." (If you are a Leonard Nimoy - *Mr Spock* fan you could try saying, "Fascinating".) Be genuinely curious – frown slightly, pause, focus your eyes on them and with a slight tilt of the head say, "Why would you say that?" or if they have threatened to take some dire action: "Why would you do that?"
- Try humor. It might work, though you have to be clever with it.

> "So, is it custard pies or pistols at dawn?"
> "You're always trying to make a joke of it."
> "Well, someone has to. But I don't mind if you have a go."

This is beginning to degenerate into farce ... Until you have perfected the art so that you both end up rolling on the floor wracked with laughter, exercise caution – and observe closely what does happen. Be careful what you say. There are several ways of putting things that probably don't help (of course, you may not want to help): "Never mind" "Oh dear." This is of course a high-status ploy, but it would be useful if you want to prevent someone from trying to dump their stuff onto you. "I've got all these extras files to work on ..." "Oh dear" puts it back onto them.

CHAPTER 35
Stress

WHAT ME WORRY?
Sometimes stress is a good thing – *eustress* – for example, the anticipation of starting a new and challenging job, participating in a sports activity or starting a new sexual relationship. Most of us, however, tend to dwell on the negative stresses in our lives – *distress*. Some relationships are forged by stress. Members of teams, military units, and so on, are united by the bond of common stressors. On the other hand, some relationships are broken apart by stress when there is evidence of dishonesty, jealously, money issues or favoritism.

On the whole, people are neurotic: they worry. Sometimes worry has a value and motivates you to take action to change something. But most of the time it just uses up mental energy on things you can't do much about. This is especially true when your worries are directed at yourself, your self-image, your expectations, your beliefs and so on. Somehow we clutter up our minds with beliefs that do us no favors; they're pernicious because they get in the way of engaging with life full on.

Following are some common irrational thoughts that cause stress in humans and tend to result in undue pressure on the bonds of relationships. I have organized these beliefs according to the four-part system I've used previously for character traits. The thing about beliefs is that they become real in your own mind, but on closer examination you realize that they are unfounded – you just made them up. You may find some old favorites here, and you could decide to challenge these beliefs, as that will affect the way you think about yourself and others for the better.

Disempowering Beliefs

There is no limit to the human imagination in finding reasons for not doing things. We are masters in excuse-making and pointing to causes beyond our control. But often these things are within our control if only we examine the belief for what it is – just a belief – and stop using these beliefs as excuses. Here are some disempowering beliefs that limit us in our lives:

- **Helplessness**. Helpless is having no options, feeling stuck because of your genes, your upbringing, your parents, the whole nature/nurture thing. It gives rise to beliefs like: "This is just the way I am – there's nothing I can do about it." "I am not capable of change." "I'll never understand this." "I do not have the power to change anything." This leads to feeling that you are a victim, unable to change the status quo.
- **Hopelessness**. Hopeless has given up at the first hurdle. Obstacles abound, and they are insurmountable. That gives rise to the belief that "Certain outcomes are just not possible." "There's just no way I can do that." "It won't work." "It doesn't make sense."
- **Worthlessness**. Worthless is putting yourself down, minimizing your status. "I am not worthy" "I'm a bad person," "I do not deserve anything." "Just ignore me; pretend I'm not here."
- **Pointlessness**. Pointless is a lack of vision, not seeing anything good in the future, nothing worth working for, so "What's the point?" "Where would it get you?" "Whatever." This way boredom lies, because there are no possibilities, no surprises.

Limiting beliefs

All of these come from a more general misunderstanding of the way the world works. Essentially, we have to learn to live with uncertainty. I mentioned this in Chapter 11. We have to learn to balance the two pulls: one towards fixing the world to make it stable; the other addresses our need to change things. Life is a series of constant adjustments in an ever-changing world. Nothing is ever perfect, at least not for long. We want things to be different; our expectations are often frustrated. If we think the world is fixed and that we are in control, we develop beliefs about how it *should* be, what *ought* to happen, When it doesn't turn out that way, we get upset.

So if you find you agree with these:
- Reality should match my expectations;
- I know what's right, what's moral, and other people should conform;
- It should be easy to make changes;
- We know what to do, so we should be able to solve problems quickly and effectively;
- Other people should approve of me, respect me, love me, just for being me;
- I don't like the idea of all this change, so I'm going to ignore i;
- I should have known what was going to happen, seen it coming …

then maybe you're a glass-half-empty kind of person. In which case, there's no hope. Kidding! Beliefs are not compulsory. As Albert Ellis used to say, "Shouldhood equals shithood" and "Stop shoulding on Yourself"! You have updated your beliefs many times during your life, so what's to stop you doing it again? No, don't bring out those tired old excuses, we've heard them all before. Stop thinking about yourself so much and do things that will raise your self-worth by putting in the effort to achieve more worthwhile things. You weren't born knowing how to do everything; you have to do the hard graft. Then you'll find the world becomes more positive, more interesting, more inspiring.

Meanwhile, for those people who love lists, here is a checklist of the symptoms of stress. Some of these you could remedy just by taking a moment to think … and then changing a behavior or two. Remember that in order to make life easy on yourself, change one thing at a time. Then you'll be able to determine the effectiveness of the change. If you change several things, you'll never be able to disentangle the causal relationships. By making only one change, there's a good chance you can.

Symptoms of Stress

- Nervous tics
- Muscular aches
- Increase (or loss) of appetite
- Increase in smoking
- Inability to sleep or nightmares
- Increased sweating
- Stuttering
- Nausea or stomach pains
- Grinding teeth
- Headaches, dizziness
- Low grade infection
- Rash or acne
- Desire to cry or crying
- Constipation or diarrhea
- Frigidity or impotence
- Loss of sex drive
- High blood pressure
  Dry mouth or throat
- Irritability or bad temper
- Lethargy or inability to work
- Cold, clammy, or clenched hands
- Sudden bursts of energy
- Restlessness, finger tapping, foot tapping, pencil tapping
- Depression
- Fear, panic, or anxiety
- Hives
- Coughing
- Excessive snacking
- Nagging

- Fatigue
- Pacing
- Frowning, wrinkling forehead
- Unnecessary hand-waving, making wild gestures.

The Visitor Problem

What happens to your level of stress when you know that
visitors are going to arrive – could be for a meal together, or
could be to stay a couple of days? How you react may depend
on gender. For men, it's usually no big deal. They will help
get ready by cleaning the house, tidying the yard, making sure
that things work, and so on. For women, it's different. When
other people come, they are seen as sitting in judgment over the
household. And everything has to be perfect; it's all about giving
the right impression, and being assessed on how well this is
done.

Trouble is that when the woman goes into preparation mode,
her personality shifts. My experience was that the only thing
that mattered was how the house was looking. I felt left out;
my wife was no longer available, so to speak. She was too
busy concentrating on getting things right that her humor
button malfunctioned and no intimate touching was permitted
– you know the sort of thing – the brief touch on the arm, the
occasional hug – all that stuff was off limits as though we were
having to behave properly in front of her parents. Part of this
tidying up was that I was part of the program – I had to be
made respectable and was warned about what not to say. In
other words, tied in with house cleaning is the woman's need
to fix men. It's their project when they get married. And it
shows whenever the couple are to be on public display. If they
eventually separate, it's because she tried her best, but the man
was obviously of inferior stock and could not be successfully
improved.

Stress-Relieving Techniques

- Love and respect yourself.
- Take time to smell the roses rather than 'pick flowers on horseback'.
- Prioritize things to be done, do one at a time, and delegate tasks for others to do. For example, if you are the kind of person who has to tidy the house before the cleaning person comes, then stop doing that. There are more important things you could be doing, so do something that will be more beneficial for you. Go to the gym or read a book.
- Give yourself plenty of time for each task – and remember that everything takes longer than you think …
- Keep fresh, keep learning.
- Learn to say Yes to opportunities, to bring variation and surprises into your life, and to avoid later regrets.
- Learn to say No to other people's demands; you can't do everything.
- Go 'Continental' for your lunch break – give yourself time; avoid the hurried sandwich at your desk.
- Go for 'good enough' rather than trying to be a perfectionist.
- Become more flexible and find new ways of doing things.
- Increase listening, decrease talking.
- Spend more time cultivating relationships with calm, steady people.
- Get up 30 minutes earlier to prepare more slowly for the day ahead.
- Set aside an hour a day to be alone and relax.
- Insist on having a time and place at home to be alone without being interrupted.

Let's look at these last two in more detail:

220 • SOME ASSEMBLY REQUIRED

Take time for yourself

Multi-tasking was one of the great cons of the last few decades.
Of course, bosses and managers thought it was great – they
wanted you working harder on a range of projects. Recently
some proper research has been done and the results show that
working on multiple projects simultaneously – well, it's not
actually simultaneous – it's more like flipping channels on a TV.
The more you do it, the more confusing it is because you have to
adjust to each new program, and that takes a lot of memory and
context sorting. Essentially it slows you down and makes you
less efficient. You get less done.

Far better is to work on one thing at a time, so that you can
really get into the flow of what you are doing. You know how
irritating it is when someone interrupts you in the middle of
your work. Why is it that many office spaces are now designed
for this to happen? Everyone needs quiet space to work. They
also need communal areas – around the water-cooler – where
they can socialize and swap ideas. Some enlightened workplaces
do acknowledge this and provide such spaces. Perhaps this is
why many people now prefer working at home – just to avoid
constant interruptions.

You also need time out from work. Working all hours is actually
bad for you; productivity drops significantly. It's not sensible
to be working all day and all evening. You boss is delusional
in thinking this increases your output. It doesn't. Better to have
frequent breaks and limited hours. Then your unconscious mind
can do its job and come up with innovative and sensible answers
to the questions you have raised in the process of getting the job
done.

"I want to be alone ..."

Do you find that you get 'peopled out'? Contact may be
stimulating, in which case you need to stop before you reach
mental overload and take a moment to digest what's been said

before it gets overwritten by other events.

You've heard the advice about sleeping on a problem. That's good advice. It's an excellent way of being creative, inspired and enthusiastic – and that's what you need to be if you are going to inspire others to be at their best.

Skills Needed To Reduce Stress

Seriously though, there are many other things you can do to reduce your stress, and the first thing to do is to identify what's causing you the stress in the first place. That will give you a clue about what to do next.

Where does the stress originate? If it's from within yourself, then all the suggestions above could be useful. Whatever you do, you need to maintain and monitor your good physical health, by developing good nutritional habits and keeping fit by engaging in vigorous regular exercise.

If it comes from the environment then those things you can fix easily – just fix them. If they are major, then consider moving, changing your commuting patterns and so on.

If it's other people, then that's what this book is about. The emphasis here is on what you personally can do, because it's not about trying to change other people. They don't like it, they'll resist. But if you start acting differently, it's very likely that they will respond to this 'new you'.

A good laugh

When was the last time you had a really good laugh? It has been shown many times that laughter is good for the health, which is why laughing clubs have been set up around the world. If you can turn your frustrations to laughter rather than anger, you stand a much better chance of having a longer and more positive relationship with someone.

Within a close relationship the amount of laughter is probably a good indicator of how strong the relationship is. If a couple can defuse tension and stress with laughter, then they're well on the way to solving the problem and strengthening their relationship.

CHAPTER 36
Work Relationships

SHARING THE LOAD
Very few jobs can be done without any contribution from others, so we join together to achieve what would be impossible by ourselves. Then you have not only the task but also the relationships between the team members to consider. That can be both satisfying and, at times, frustrating.

A team ideally consists of a number of people who have various skills working together towards a specific outcome, for example, a Hollywood film crew, a theater company putting on a show. The focus is on setting goals, arranging timetables, defining roles (who does what by when, the way each person is to be held accountable for the outcomes, and how feedback is given), identifying and overcoming any barriers that can be anticipated, supporting the efforts of others in the group. All these things, when done in a collaborative manner, will build trust between the individuals. This trust (earned through reliability – doing what you say you're going to do) will build the bond required in a good short-term relationship.

Acute ad hoc Relationships
Sometimes a group of people is brought together for a very short time – a few hours, a day or two – to solve a problem. Then they disperse. That means you need to know how to manage temporary, acute relationships where you have to bond quickly in order to get things done. Essentially, you initially focus on the task, the intention, the goal, and hope that in the process bonding will occur. In other words, you focus on everything that isn't the relationship at first and the rest will follow. On a good day.

If things start to veer off-course – some people get caught up in what they think they are meant to be doing (an example of hooking) or are impatient to start doing, rather than thinking things through or planning – then what's needed is a reminder of what you are there to do. Unless the goal is really obvious, it's a good idea to write up the specified outcomes where everyone can see them. Then it's easier to challenge any deviation by pointing at the list. That saves you from taking personal responsibility for managing the group.

Group structure

Over time, groups naturally organize themselves into something that works reasonably well. Or at least, they work for the initial purpose the group has been set up for. However, there is no guarantee that the particular way it has organized itself is going to be the best for any further projects.

It's usually the case that a team is exceptional with one kind of project but hopeless with another. It may have an expert who can guide the team in making a particular decision, but when the project shifts its focus, no team member has sufficient knowledge. Context matters. Each team is unique, each has its own pace and rhythm, so any outside forces requiring them to change can be a recipe for disaster.

One danger is that the members of the group who have attained higher status and who organize things want to keep their structure, because for them it defines their place in the hierarchy. In other words, the structure – the hierarchy – becomes self-serving. This is only natural. People want stability and yet it is only available on a temporary basis, regardless of how much we would like things to stay the same. Everything fails or collapses, given enough time. A better mindset is for people to accept uncertainty, and to be flexible, able to adapt quickly and to let go of what no longer serves them, however comfortable it once was.

Whatever your role in the team, you need to manage or at least be aware of all the different relationships. Ideally, this should be an enjoyable process because you want to be with these other people (but not all the time; you need space for yourself as well) and the never-ending process of getting to know them more deeply. The better you get to know the other people, the easier the team becomes at making decisions. You know each other's strengths, preferences, styles, and types, so you can assign the scepter accordingly.

Joining an existing group
There is an art to joining a group, a society, a team, an organization, if you want things to run smoothly. There are strategies for integrating into your new team or place of work. Every group develops its own way of being. When someone applies for membership, the group's task is to make sure the newcomer knows 'how we do things here'. They will need time, and often help, to absorb the culture. The team needs to be sure that they will fit in to the team culture, rather than rock the boat – though at times, a good shake-up will be exactly what the team needs.

Some groups or teams build their affiliation by making the novice undergo some kind of ritual initiation process. This could be as mild as giving them the company rule book to read or there could be some kind of bizarre ritual designed to humiliate the candidate in front of the group by lowering their status to the absolute minimum. The greater the humiliation, the greater their loyalty will be. However, this should not be degrading or injurious – hazing is not permissible.

The right person for the job?
Interviews are notoriously unreliable. What people say can vary widely from what they are able to do. How they come across at an interview is not a good predictor of how effective

they will be. So if you are recruiting newcomers into the team or group, it's a good idea to test them out at the job they are going to be doing and also to test out their response to being given feedback. Do they appreciate it? Do they enthusiastically learn from experience? You need to check this before finally committing anything, just to see how well they will fit into the already established culture of the group. Also check whether they actually want to join this particular group. It may not be for them.

Once people feel that they belong to the group, they are more likely to support it and influence other team-members to be equally supportive and hard working. That is, to join the group requires the expression of commitment (rather like marriage vows). The result is the feeling that you don't want to let the side down yourself, and you expect others to feel and behave the same way.

So if you are the person joining a team, realize that it will take time to fully understand the dynamics, the relationships, the culture. Take time to familiarize yourself with the way the team works, find out what's expected of you. Find an ally of whom you can ask questions. You may need to begin by lowering your status "I'm new here, and I'd really like to know ..." Whether you choose to question the underlying ethos – what we're all about – is up to your assessment of the risks and possible benefits.

CHAPTER 37
Teams

"We start from the assumption that our people are talented and want to contribute. We accept that, without meaning to, our company is stifling that talent in myriad unseen ways. Finally, we try to identify those impediments and fix them."
~ ED CATMULL (2014) *Creativity, Inc,* p. xv

O K, SO YOU ARE NOW part of a team. You've been through the various stages of coming together, and now you can focus on getting things done – which is the reason you're here. Although the following guidelines apply to every team, it's also the case that every team will be different.

Teaming up
There are five elements of teaming that tend to bring (and bond) people together. These are:
- *A set of agreed-upon goals and objectives.* These allow you to focus on the task.
- *Clearly defined roles and responsibilities.* You are clear about who is responsible, for what, by when, and how are we going to check with each other to make sure we're on track.
- *Identification of any barriers* that may get in your way preventing you from achieving your goals.
- *Support mechanisms: leadership, feedback, membership requirements.* You will benefit from regular feedback so that you can make adjustments along the way.
- *Good and continuous communication* based on the four communication styles we've discussed above – Driver, Expressive, Amiable, Analytical – together with all of the

other factors, like introversion/extroversion differences for each of these four.

Working Well Together

In a little more detail, to have the group working well together, it's worth bearing in mind the dynamics and composition of the team. It's better to have a mixture of types in a team. Don't select people all of the same type. You don't want a team composed of dominant leader types – they just won't get on together; a team of Drivers will drive each other crazy. You could divide up team tasks based upon personalities. For example, you probably don't want to give an auditing task to someone who has an Expressive personality. They could do the job, sort of, but the results would be questionable. Instead, it's better to give this auditing task to an Analytical personality, since they can do the job without any stress. Be careful, though, with your assumptions about the different types. For example, you may be dealing with an introverted Expressive person, someone who walks down the hallway with a light step and continuous smile. They may not say much (or acknowledge another person's presence), but inside their head they're having a fiesta. Or you may be dealing with an extroverted Analytical who chases you down the hallway spouting facts and figures at you like a machine gun until you just want to choke the life out of them.

Barriers to Working Well

There's no lack of factors that harm or impede good working relationships. Here are just a few. To start with, think of Herzberg's Hygiene factors: a lack of funds, inadequate pay, lack of (working) equipment, an unpleasant space in which to work.

There also needs to be benevolent management, people who support and work with teams rather than exercising a dictatorship, or any form of micromanagement. In general, the teams need a level of autonomy, with limited external control/ constraints. Remember whom you're doing this for.

The team needs to be up-to-date with best working practices and to have high expectations of what can be achieved. This needs to be reflected by those in power in the organization. In terms of planning, the traditional waterfall model – planning in detail over the long-term – is neither effective nor efficient, because things will always deviate from plan from the moment the ink has dried. The team needs frequent feedback, testing and checking that what has been done so far actually works.

It's not just the Christmas Office party, but social relationships within the group that can interfere with the work. This is especially so if team-members focus more on creating relationships with other team members. That's not what you are there for. And it's probably a bad idea.

Join the club
You choose your friends and your spouse (chronic relationships) voluntarily because of the attraction you have for the other person's values (as displayed by their behaviors and the words they use). To that extent we can choose whom to associate with, but usually, when you take up a post in an organization – and you've already checked them out as far as possible at an interview – you don't have a lot of say about who your colleagues will be. You are allocated to a specific work team, probably an ad hoc group (acute relationship group formed for a specific purpose). Once the purpose/goal has been achieved, the team disperses and the members may never meet each other again.

It may also be a good career move to join the preferred social group outside of work – where the people at work spend some of their leisure time. My son Max joined a philanthropic fraternity in college and spent time working on projects with them. After he graduated, the only contact he's had with them is the occasional newsletter he receives. The bond was brief and focused. Then it was gone. The same can be said for nearly all acute relationships. This includes churches where people have an initial bond based on a loose set of similar values, but the bond more easily breaks when values shift or someone doesn't like the priest/pastor/rabbi or the political nature of the organization gets in the way. It's also possible that the individual's need has by then been satisfied, and it's time to move on. If the need was not satisfied, then people look elsewhere, seeking a new set of bonds to make with other groups ... looking for a stronger longer-term bond for mental/emotional stability.

After all, mental/physical comfort is the purpose of all bonding in both acute and chronic relationships. It's just more difficult to achieve in acute, short-term, relationships. Friendships take time, especially as you get older, and do require some positive action on your part.

It's been said that familiarity breeds contempt. That may be true, but not always. If you've had a good acute relationship with someone, perhaps on a work group or club, and the break happens, if the opportunity to join together again occurs the bond is created quicker and stronger ... because of familiarity. Meeting up with old colleagues often brings back good memories of past shared experiences. Unless, of course, you had a bad experience working with someone. In that case, the bond was never formed to begin with.

Take a moment to think about how you reinvented yourself and re-presented yourself in a variety of groups that you either had to join, or chose to join.
- Which aspects of yourself did you deliberately change?
- How did that change how you felt about yourself? Did you like the different you?
- How did that affect other people around you?

CHAPTER 38

Decision Making

MAKING DECISIONS IS A KEY activity with every group and can often be extremely challenging. Deciding alone can be fraught, but decision-making might seem easier when working collectively with a team because the burden is shared, or so it seems. But this is an illusion. Someone, one person, has to take responsibility for the decision that's made. The team is there to help the leader make that decision, and the leader has to commit to a course of action, with or without the whole team's approval.

Ideally, every team member should have equal status when it comes to proposing a solution. Bias is likely to occur if individuals are swayed by the leader's opinion or by majority views (which could be wrong or sub-optimal). It's often the case that a single member is the only one with the correct solution and they need to be heard and allowed to explain their choice. When you explain your solution, talk in terms of:

- Why this particular solution. (Start with 'why' because that sets the scene.)
- Explain what it is, and more importantly, what it does, what effect it has.
- Then look at how it can be used to make the changes you desire.
- Explore possible consequences, what could be done that's not possible to do now.
- Also cover potential hazards, unwanted results and how to overcome them.

If you follow this outline, the listeners should be able to visualize or imagine your idea put into action. Essentially you are telling a story – and everyone likes stories.

It's a good idea to only allow criticism of any particular choice only after all ideas have been expressed. Even though it's sometimes hard to listen to ideas that are not your own, knowing that you are not going to respond immediately makes it easier to pay attention without rehearsing what you want to say.

Can you see this solution working? If you are unable to imagine putting this plan into action, how it could possibly work, then seek clarification.

Not every idea survives to become part of the finished product. So don't treat your idea as your baby that has to be protected at all costs. What you think is a good idea will probably not meet someone else's criteria. Get used to failure by creating several ideas and releasing them into the pool, knowing that many of them won't survive this round of activity. They may disappear completely or they could reemerge in a different context. It's a case of survival of the fittest against competing ideas.

There are seven different decision-making methods available that individuals/teams can use on their path towards achieving outcomes. These are:

1.   *Consensus*. This reduces the risk for all members but results in mediocre outcomes at best. It takes a long time to weigh all the options, the goal of which is to avoid disagreements.

2.   *Majority vote*. One person, one vote. It's quick, decisive, and potentially political. It's what we're used to.

3.   *Minority vote*. This is where no one knows the answers or has the expertise to figure it out. It requires a small group of people to go ask others who know more about the subject, then take their findings back to the group for discussion and resolution.

4.   *Averaging*. This is an example of the wisdom of crowds – where you take everyone's best guess and calculate

the average, or you put everyone's ideas on the table and look for the mode (the most frequently chosen point). The problem is that you can have more than one most frequently chosen point – at which point you can either toss a coin – or you can engage in debate (and then possibly suffer from turf wars).

5.   *Expert*. This is where you hire someone from the outside who tells you what you already know but charges you for it so you believe their opinions more than your own … like couples counseling … or consultants.

6.   *Authority Rule Without Discussion*. This is where the one in power says, "Do it my way or else." Input from others is not required or requested. Best used in emergencies when you don't really have the time for discussions (like during fires). The one in power takes over and gives commands. No discussions, just do it. Once the emergency is over, the postmortem begins, together with the incriminations.

7.   *Authority With Discussion*. For each goal, a prime decision-maker is identified and agreed upon by the group. They make any final decision based on the input from people both inside and outside the group. Once they have enough information to make a decision, they stop the process, make the decision, and provide feedback to all who have inputted information to let them know how their information has contributed to the final decision.

Finding your niche

You're good at things other people are not so good at. That's why you were hired. In the team you get satisfaction from demonstrating your skills and expertise. Other people are the same. Therefore, a good plan is to find out – either by observation or by asking – what turns them on, what floats their boat. In any team or relationship you need complementary skills, and you need to know when someone else is better at you at doing something. It's OK not to be number one. Recognizing someone else's expertise gives them support – they like to talk about what they do to someone who understands – and that helps build the relationship.

Status and competence are fluid concepts; you are all floating up and down the scale all the time. Think of the relationships where you are always one-down. Is that relationship fun? Is it likely to change? Would you like to walk away from it? Guess so, if you could do so, without losing too much else.

Fear of losing intellectual property

You are expected to contribute your wisdom to the group. You share what you know because to some extent the other team members depend on your expertise – as you depend on theirs. You may fear that you are giving it away. It took you years to acquire your knowledge and competence, and now you are expected to short-cut it for them by giving it all away. Do not be concerned. Either they will erect a monument to you or they will do their best to take what you give and run with it. This, after all, is your reward. But no one can take away your learning process and the value it has given you. You might think that others can simply get what you have got, but they can't. There's no way you can acquire someone's years of experience in becoming expert; you can only benefit from the consequences. Think of the reason you did all that work – it was to pass on your knowledge, wasn't it? Nor be afraid that others will overtake you – they won't catch up with all your ideas, because you've been thinking about them longer, from your own perspective. They may be able to take additional steps and they will then acknowledge your contribution. Same way you did with their ideas. Learning from others is a two-way process, and it brings with it respect of different points of view and levels of expertise.

Social Loafing

By contrast, there are some who contribute only a little. Are you pulling your weight in the group? Because the team takes responsibility, that means responsibility is shared, and however much you do, you still get the accolades the team gets. If you're not contributing your fair share, perhaps you're in the wrong team, and it would be better to be doing something where you felt valued. If so, then it's time to draw attention to this. Being open and honest is an essential part of group dynamics. It's not necessary to leave the group; there are other options, and one of them is to throw it open to the group that you have this problem to resolve. That's what a good group is for.

Information Hoarding

Another negative trait is to have someone in the group who is information hoarding. That is, they know things but they're not sharing, to the detriment of the team. This is the kind of game that rival departments engage in; either through malice or incompetence, they fail to share what they know with others who need the information (think Pearl Harbor). Sooner or later – and it could be years later – they'll be found out. If you find this in a team, best remove the person for not playing the game. They have to go, because being a team member is not about making yourself indispensable. That information hoarder has a hidden agenda – which won't include you, other than to use you for their ends. You have to able to trust everyone in the team. Once someone's predilection for hoarding data gets known, others in the group will no longer trust them with any further information.

CHAPTER 39

Affiliation Groups

The key to building relationships – join the Masons!

THREE'S A CROWD
For many years there has been a general trend of moving from the country to the city. In the process, one of the things we lose is the connection to the people around us. When there are relatively few people, it's easy to get to know them. In the 1990s, the British anthropologist Robin Dunbar worked out that on average human beings can comfortably manage about 150 stable relationships. If you work in a large organization or live in a village or small community you should be able to verify that from your own experience. In practice, with working groups, once the 150-member group is exceeded, it becomes beneficial to split them and continue with two smaller groups. A prime example is that of the company W. L. Gore and Associates, known now for the *Gore-Tex* brand, who discovered, by trial and error, that if the staff increased to more than 150 employees then problems would occur, and the best solution was to then split the staff into two by building another site where they could work.

Although nowadays it is very easy to count your friends on Facebook or other social media in the hundreds, when you take a realistic look at whom you are connected to, how many significant relationships can you identify? Probably not even 150 – that's based on casually bumping into people around the village or the office and knowing their names and a little bit about them. How many true friends do you have? Be honest. Be surprised at how few there really are. (There are some of us who collect relationships in the same way that others collect baseball cards – and the enthusiasm for any particular card will last as long as it lasts – that is, it will soon be superseded.)

If three's a crowd, so how about seven billion? That's how many people there are on the planet. But we are picky. Within that multitude, we choose to spend most of our time with a very select few. But we also need variety, stimulation of different kinds, so we join with others for a variety of purposes and goals. Whether it's through common experiences, such as the VFW where all members served in combat overseas or through common purpose, the Masonic/Shriners' Hospitals, or through common values, like churches/synagogues ... held together by prayer but separated by practice/liturgy, we all seek like-minded yet unique individuals with whom to affiliate so we don't feel like we are on this earth alone.

It starts with people. Normally, folks don't just wake up one morning and say, "I'm going to put on an apron, a set of moose antlers and a chain out of King Arthur's court." They strike up casual conversations with friends and coworkers who invite the curious to visit a meeting or gathering of the potentially like-minded. After all, new blood is always welcome, since time and alternative priorities often sap the ranks of the vested. A bit of fun, some camaraderie, a common attractive purpose, and before you know it, you're wearing the ring. Some of these organizations bear the test of time with their good deeds, national reputations and the fame of former members. Others dissolve when the beer runs out.

The need for affiliation is very strong within the human spirit. People are drawn to each other like moths to a flame. Even in these days of mobile communications and social networks, face-to-face contact still has top priority. People are prepared to travel long distances to attend seminars or just to be together on special occasions. Even though we celebrate our uniqueness, we also like to share interests and seek common ground among like-minded others. It's about having a sense of belonging and avoiding feeling isolated from society. In order to encounter these like-minded souls, we have established a number of sorting systems – named groups, associations, organizations, clubs, societies, communities … all of which enable us to build our social networks. Indeed, our society has pre-planned one of these organizations to which subscription is obligatory – the school. Within the school system, we then find smaller groups to which we choose to belong – the choir, the sports teams, the after-school interest clubs for insects, plays, debates and so on. By the time we are adults, we have had plenty of experience of moving in and out of such groups and have established a lifetime habit. Adult society offers a great deal more; the wider the community you live in, the greater the potential range of stimulation.

Another benefit of being in regular contact with your social circle is that you are more aware of what's going on, what other people are doing, and what they need. You have opportunities for helping or contributing. And there is some degree of reciprocity; they will help you as well, so that in the end, everyone benefits. This is not necessarily on a financial transaction basis but a matter of general neighborliness.

The Social Resume

One of the first things we do when meeting strangers, apart from assessing their relative status, is to find out what we have in common. Starting with your home town, because where you live often confers status upon you – think Detroit or The Hamptons, for example. Your social standing also relates to any particular group, organization, or club you belong to, similarly your school or college. Think how attending an Ivy League university can benefit.

This is about finding short-cuts for understanding the other person. We like to be with people like ourselves, who have had similar histories, similar life experiences – because this makes connecting easier – we speak the same language. Finding shared interests – sports, games, hobbies and pastimes – means you can compare golf handicaps or discuss different camera makes, and this increases the level of bonding. Same thing if you've shared similar life-changing experiences – war, disaster, illness; it's our way of making contact with alien beings.

Fez of a feather

And this leads to the formation of *affiliation groups*. By that I mean any religious organization, any fraternity or sorority, alumni organization, any social, political, activist group, and so on. These have all arisen from our need to associate with others around common values.

Let's take a peek at some of the statistics. According to David Barrett, et al, editors of the *World Christian Encyclopedia: A comparative survey of churches and religions – AD 30 to 2200*, there are 19 major world religions which are subdivided into a total of 270 large religious groups and many smaller ones. Thirty-four thousand separate Christian groups have been identified in the world. "Over half of them are independent churches that are not interested in linking with the big denominations. There are also some 250 fraternities/sororities registered in the US, depending on who's sober when the counting took place, as well as over 1500 social affiliations like the Masons, Knights of Columbus, Knights of Pythias, Independent Order of Odd Fellows, The Grange, The Elks, The Moose, the Woodmen and my uncle's favorite, the Keepers of the Secret Spittoon … 1500 of them. That should tell you something. What it tells me is about our need to be with others; to still exercise our uniqueness, but within a common group mindset. Even the evil-doers of extremist behaviors, where the shared belief is that the world would be a far better place if they were to rid it of people not like themselves, still find ways of making themselves unique from other groups with similar aims – "you slice the neck right to left while we do it left to right, so we're different/better."

If you were to make a list of all the groups you have ever been in, it would probably be quite long and would reflect your changing attitudes, desires and interests over the years. Each affiliation group serves its purpose for a time. Some we grow out of, others we lose interest in as our priorities change. In the process of having and rearing children, different groups come into view because we continue to want to be with people like ourselves who are sharing similar experiences.

So why did you join in the first place? Was it to gain a better understanding of some specific content or learn a skill? Or perhaps you wanted to meet other people, with a view to making new friends?

People tend to be much more mobile these days – for example, moving to be near other members of the family, or because of job changes, or just for a change of scenery. That means having to start again building up social networks. You may have one or two to start with, but you need to get out there and find others.

Establishing and building strong relationships within affiliation groups is sort of a combination of the need to build friendships while also dealing with the protocols and politics required at work.

Come and join us!
So you want to build up the pool of acquaintances in order to find those special people. If you've just arrived in a new town or city, how do you get to meet others? Chance encounters are fine but by definition cannot be arranged to order. So when opportunities do arise, make contact. For example, if you are a keen photographer and you spot someone else wielding a camera, go and talk to them. You'll soon find out whether you get along. You'll either be enthusiastically swapping notes

or wishing each other the time of day. Either way, you are validating the other person by acknowledging their choice of hobby, activity, interest.

Join any groups that take your fancy. You've very little to lose – because meeting new people can be an entertainment in itself. If you are a bit shy … well, take the advice given earlier: just do it. Even when you imagine other people are going to perceive you as this or that, you're probably exaggerating – they don't really know you, they can't read your innermost thoughts, and, anyway, they are willing to greet you warmly and welcome you in because that's what we do. It's something we've all been through, so we know what it's like. Trust the moment. Play low status at first, and people will explain things, tell you things, look after you until you have become acclimated to the group atmosphere.

Pressure to stay or pressure to go?

Some groups put pressure on you to stay a member. Sometimes the group itself makes it clear that you no longer fit in with their ethics, purpose, culture, especially if you want to update them or have them change in some way. Changing a whole group is hard. Changing one person is a mighty challenge, but to go up against collective values, whew! We have to thank Charles M. Schulz for: "No problem is so big or so complicated that it can't be run away from!" Far better to spend your time and energy working on and improving yourself, building relationships that are reciprocated and are creative and fun. Very few informal groups ask you directly to leave; but that does happen in formal groupings, work situations and long-established clubs. Because being part of a group entails some reciprocal commitment – caring goes both ways.

Upholding the group's values and principles is a minimum requirement – most groups give you a trial period of membership just to see whether you're going to turn it into a long-term relationship. There's little point in having members who subvert the intentions of the society; they will leave it to your judgment to know whether to go or stay. If you pay an annual subscription, then you are not committed beyond your natural interest. You've given it a fair trial; does it still meet your original need?

Don't we just love living with opposing desires! We both seek the comfort of groups as well as seeking to have our uniqueness appreciated. Somehow, we find a way of managing these opposing needs. But when we can't quite manage to suppress our personal values in order to 'conform' to the group values, then turnover takes place. This is another example of cognitive dissonance, that internal pressure we feel when trying to rectify the difference between personal preference/values and the group preference. People leave groups (and seek other groups) when they find it too hard to fit their personal values into the values of the group.

This is also my theory on one of the origins of PTSD. People go into battle, say, with a sense of duty to country. They must do what they are trained to do in combat. But then reality sets in and they take actions that are contrary to their personal values. Thou Shall Not Kill, for example, does not fit well in battle. When they come home, the conflict between their internal values and their external behaviors is sometimes too much to take, resulting in some form of PTSD (post-traumatic stress disorder). Doing what you've been raised not to do creates such pressure internally that it can become really hard to compartmentalize your thinking and justify the actions you've taken. PTSD is the result.

There is an unspoken pressure to stay inside a group once you become a member. No group likes to lose people – it suggests there might be something wrong with it: "What's the matter? Why don't you like us?" Some fraternities, for example, put novices through such humiliating pledge practices that these embarrassing situations bind you to your other 'brothers' who have suffered similar fate. The fraternal orders in English universities would add to the bonding process by making sure all members would wear some symbol of the organization making them recognizable to others of their sect … the ties that bind.

I remember many years ago when I started working for Burlington Northern Railroad after four years working for the government. I was a Manager of Personnel Research and Development which meant I needed to interact with many people at many levels within the company. These are all long-term tough railroad guys. No one paid me much attention since I was young, well-educated (a PhD) and on a tear to change the culture … at least move the needle a bit. No matter how hard I tried, no one would give me the time of day. One day, sitting across the desk from my boss, I noticed a ring he had on his finger with an interesting symbol on it. I inquired what it represented. He said it was a Masonic ring. He also told me something very interesting. He told me that no one would help me if I didn't have a similar ring on my finger. I noticed that most if not all of the upper management and nearly all of the old timers had similar rings … of different designs. Then my boss told me that if I wanted, he would sponsor me on the road to becoming a Mason … if I wanted. The hint was as bright as the lights at the Flamingo Casino in Las Vegas. I said yes. Over the next several months, I went to all the Masonic training sessions … became a Mason (33rd degree), kept the secrets of the temple and got my ring. It was amazing. Once I had the ring on my finger it was as if I could do no wrong. People went out of their way to help me initiate the changes I wanted to see take place within the company. Resources became available that were denied me before. It was a clear sign of the benefits of affiliation. I was with the in-crowd. That, of course, didn't guarantee that I got done what I wanted. I was still that snot-nosed young PhD. There were still political hurdles to overcome and people in power that needed convincing … but at least I was given an audience. I did what I had to do to be accepted by the powers in the organization. Every organization has circles of power that you may need to learn to penetrate, using affiliations as a pry bar.

CHAPTER 40
Time to Move On

WHEN THE ROUGH RUFFLES THE smooth
In every context – home, work, leisure, affiliation group – there comes a time when staying together is no longer an option. Perhaps your planned discussions have been too one-sided and the other person is stonewalling or blaming you. Or they may have decided that they want out but have not been upfront in telling you. You have reached a stage where any attempt at remediation goes nowhere; pointing out any deficiency leads to a shouting match, and never a kind word passes between you.

Hostility is just another word for immaturity. It seems easier to let go than to do the hard work of stitching a tattered relationship together. You can't (or don't know how) to stop being angry or mean to each other. If you've fallen into the habit of hostility then you need to give each other a break. Own up to your own part in this mutually destructive relationship. Stop trying to break the will of the other person. You could even just walk away.

I know of no relationship, be it a friendship or marriage, that is smooth sailing over the long haul. While peaceful co-existence is the goal, rough seas are a part of life. How you deal with each other during these harder times, when arguments and disagreements are common and unresolved, will determine whether your relationship will last. Some relationships end up stronger as a result; others fail.

The psychologist John Gottman found four key factors (which he calls the Four Horsemen of the Apocalypse – Gottman &

Silver, 2015) in his study of how to predict whether a given relationship would last: criticism of the partner's personality, contempt (from a position of superiority, and that includes eye-rolling), defensiveness, and stonewalling or emotional withdrawal from interaction. In other words, a breakdown in communication. The dominant partner defines or shows contempt for the other person: "You're a lousy lay", "You're always taking sides with your mother." "You never were good enough!" If challenged, their way of responding is not to respond; they won't let anything in nor give anything out. As such, there is no effective way of sorting out issues or resolving difficulties. Once this situation has been reached, the relationship is probably doomed.

No Put-downs

Culturally, we like to joke about, rag, insult other people. It's something we learn to do as a way of raising our status. Humor comes from applying this to ourselves; when we do this to others, it's not so funny. When anyone complains, we retort "Can't you take a joke?" Only it's not really a joke. It's a cheap ploy. In fact, many US/UK schools now have a no-putdown (and no bullying) policy; this negative behavior is not tolerated. These policies resulted from the shocking rise in suicides among young people unequipped to tolerate the downward pressure applied from others who were exerting higher status.

Although it may have become habitual, especially within certain groups, finding negative things to say could indicate a fear of change, a desire to maintain the status quo. It shows a lack of empathy. Is raising your status so important? Consider not denigrating other people. Remember when other people did it to you. How did you feel as the target? As a life strategy, demeaning, belittling, ragging other people is really a sign of one's own immaturity. You may find it somewhat limiting should you want to expand your social circle.

Making and Losing Friends

There are some obvious criteria for deciding whether to stay in a particular relationship – either with one individual or with a group. If people are continually insulting you or bullying you, then where is the threshold for deciding "No more"? How much antagonism can you tolerate? Can you forgive or overlook some of the things they do? Is there anything that is unforgivable? When changes in a relationship are incremental, it's not always easy to notice when you have crossed the threshold. You may have a lot invested in keeping a malfunctioning relationship going, especially if there are children or property involved. Leaving is never an easy thing to do.

Your decision to stay or leave, could, of course, depend on the benefit you derive from being in that group more than from the relationships. For example, I've just received a message from one group wondering why I've not renewed my subscription. I'm questioning whether I will. Do I need that group any longer? Did it give me what I wanted? And have I now got that? It's time to weigh the pros and cons and decide if it's time to move on. This is what we frequently do with our attachments – some are loose, others tight. Ask yourself: If I stopped going to this group, would I miss it? And would they miss me?

In most societies, there is a great deal of give and take, where you value what being in the group gives you and they value your contribution – and they definitely would miss you. For example, you may have been in a particular group for some years. You've served time there, learned the ropes, took on a significant role such as treasurer or events organizer and became somewhat indispensable – so the others think. But the glory has faded, and there are other things you'd rather be doing. Now is the time to think Succession Planning, so you'll able to pass on the mantel to a worthy successor. You've done your bit and you want to bow out gracefully in the near future. You're grateful for the opportunity to feel involved and useful, but it's time to go. And that's what we do frequently with our attachments – some are loose, others tight.

However, if you belong to a group that seems to take rather than give, then you might think that your so-called friends are abusing your good nature. If they are contributing little to the relationship, is this worth continuing with?

Shall I stay or shall I go?

Some people can make a clean break, though just walking out is never quite that easy. The break needs time to plan, to negotiate and the resilience to walk away without (too many) regrets. Others find that the regrets, the "if only's", keep getting in the way. These can turn to resentment and even revenge. Blame is heaped on the other person.

All that yelling at each other is not going to turn the clock back. You yell at each other in frustration, because there is no resolution and little hope of exploring options. Perhaps you are now hoping the other person will quit the relationship first so you can blame them and avoid the joint responsibility that comes with relationship failure.

Others have a bipolar response, unable to balance the desire to be somewhere else with the emotional turmoil of staying with the other person. They may be heard to say, "I'd do anything to get him back." Really? Anything? Surely it's too late by now. Better to adopt the attitude: When it's gone, it's gone. "I wish I could go back to how it was before…" No you don't. When you think about it, all that would do would stick you in a time loop where you'd be doomed to repeat the same mistakes over and over. And there'd be no escape.

The Sunk Cost Fallacy

You need to know when to call time, when to cut your losses. What you don't want is to throw good money after bad. People stay in relationships that aren't going anywhere because of what they have contributed to it in the past and they don't want to lose that. This is known as the 'sunk cost'. You have indeed invested time and energy (and money) in building a relationship that has now run its course. It's not like a bank balance, where the value somehow remains. What you paid was the price of admission; there are no refunds. Maybe now, with hindsight, you think you were taken advantage of, that overall it wasn't worth it – but during the time the relationship existed, from an objective point of view, you were fully engaged and finding out a lot about yourself and about that particular relationship. Again, there is no Undo button to press. You can't go back and choose a different option. But you can take the learning you got, change what you do and try again in a future relationship. It's not a failure even though it didn't work out how you wished. You didn't waste your time. You shared experiences; you learned from one another; then exited stage left.

"Back to Square One"

Having left, you have to start again … again. Does it get easier with practice? Not really. You still have to make many adjustments and that includes examining your life, clarifying your life's purpose one more time. But don't imagine you're back at square one because you have moved on, gained experience, are now more knowledgeable about the world and about people.

Sometimes starting again gives you an opportunity for deciding what's really important in your life and what can be discarded. Lighter in load, with more choice, more effective strategies and knowing more things that don't work, you'll be able to move ahead. And laugh a bit more often.

FINALE
The Seven Secrets of Building Lasting Relationships

1.   No one is perfect. Admit your mistakes, ask for forgiveness, and work together on problem solving.

2.   Divide your roles and responsibilities and ask Who's Responsible for What, by When, and How Are We Going to Check to See If We're On Track.

3.   Respect the opinions of your partner. Everyone has specific strengths and weaknesses. Opinions emerge from those strengths and past experiences. It's not a zero-sum game. It's possible for both of you to be right.

4.   Identify potential barriers to mutual (or individual) happiness and work on solutions together. Find common interests.

5.   Talk more about your dreams and desires for the future.

6.   Find ways to laugh together more often.

7.   When you don't know, say, "I don't know."

About the Authors

We're both boomers and this is our perspective on how things appear to us, given our lifetime experiences and how the changes in the way people relate to one another have adjusted over the last sixty years. We do our best to keep up and understand the millennials ... we have millennial kids, but forgive us if we have a slightly distant view, because we already have enough going on in our lives.

On a personal note, we have had very different experiences of relationships, as you might expect. One of us, Harvey, has been married for 35 years; On the other hand, Peter has had a series of relationships lasting varying lengths of time. Are we reasonably typical of our generation? Do we expect to have several significant relationships in our lives, kind of like the number of addresses we live at?

Given our limited sampling of living with other people in close proximity, does this make us experts on relationships? Probably not; longevity is not the point. What matters is shared interest, shared progress, a shared journey if you like. It's how we engage in our journey through life that matters. That means having a flexible way of dealing with whatever life throws at us. To cope well requires a toolbox for finding solutions to the challenges that arise. This toolbox we will share with you.

What we have in common is a background in psychology (Harvey is a practicing psychologist and Peter a seasoned observer and writer) and an ongoing desire and curiosity to understand how we make sense of our own lives and those of others. This comes by observing our behaviors and interactions with other people. We have learned a lot – and continue to learn – about what works and what doesn't work when it comes to building and maintaining relationships. Many relationships are ephemeral, and we, like you, have plenty of experience finishing them when they have run their course. Relationships end. There is no law of the universe which says a particular relationship has to last a lifetime. Despite best intentions, the relationship runs out of steam; there is nowhere either of us wants to explore further. Arriving at the end of a relationship does not signify failure (although it may seem so at the time of the break-up), merely an indication that it's time to move on by moving apart. That's not being callous; it's being realistic. There is little point in continuing a one-sided relationship which is not being reciprocated.

One important aspect of relationships is that we have a good one with ourselves. How well have you gotten to know yourself over the years? And how accurate or realistic is that view? In this book, we'll provide some ways of getting to know yourself better.

We're both old enough to have gone through the revolution in personal psychology during the 1970s and later when the post-war generation – the boomers – shrugged off the restrictive thinking of the pre-war past, and began to explore humanity and human nature in a multitude of ways. Many were innovative and misguided. (Whatever happened to Primal Scream and Encounter groups? Yeah, there are some addicts who could not let go.). Because the human psyche is resilient we got through those experimental years without lasting damage. In the process we found out what didn't work and acquired a great deal of wisdom on how to detect BS when it's presented as the latest fad or wonder-cure. We've become experts in snake-oil detection.

Some ideas are sticky. In the eternal quest to innovate and do something new in order to improve the lot of mankind a number of basic models get recycled, rebadged, re-issued to a new and needy public. There is no shortage of people who want to grab the latest understanding of what it means to be human. Alas they seem unable to make the connection with the past and with the tradition in self-help going back millennia. You are no doubt familiar with the idea that there is nothing new under the sun. It's the same old, same old, relabeled and presented as 'an idea whose time has come'. Some of these movements or ideologies will indeed take hold; whilst others will burn brightly for a while, and then disappear into a dark hole. What remains is the fundamental mystery of human relationships. What changes is the way we think about them and describe them. So for starters, we're with Joseph Campbell who said, "Life is not a problem to be solved but a mystery to be lived." Every relationship is to a large extent a mystery to be explored. If relationships were a solvable puzzle then life would become a lot less interesting!

Bibliography and References

Alter, Adam (2013) *Drunk Tank Pink: The Subconscious Forces That Shape How We Think, Feel, And Behave*, London, Oneworld Publications.

Barrett, David; Kurian, George; & Johnson, Todd (eds) (2001) *World Christian Encyclopedia: A Comparative Survey of Churches and Religions in The Modern World*, Oxford, Oxford University Press.

Baumeister, Roy & Bushman, Brad (2014) *Social Psychology and Human Nature, 3rd edition*, Belmont CA, Wadsworth, Cengage Learning.

Bridge, Gillian (2016) *The Significance Delusion*, Carmarthen, Crown House Publishing.

Burkeman, Oliver (2015) Could you be the next Mark Zuckerberg? *The Guardian* 6 November 2015 http://www.theguardian.com/lifeandstyle/2015/nov/06/zuckerberg-facebook-next-big-idea

Catmull, Ed (2014) *Creativity, Inc: overcoming the unseen forces that stand in the way of inspiration*, New York, Random House.

Chabris, Christopher & Simons, Daniel (2011) *The Invisible Gorilla: How our intuitions deceive us*, New York, Random House.

Crusco April H. & Wetzel, Christopher G.(1984) *The Midas Touch: the effects of interpersonal touch on restaurant tipping.* Pers Soc Psychol Bull 10(4): 512–517.

Ekman, Paul (2007) *Emotions Revealed, Second Edition: Recognizing Faces and Feelings to Improve Communication and Emotional Life,* New York, Henry Holt & Company, 2nd edition.

Festinger, Leon (1957) *A Theory of cognitive dissonance.* Stanford, CA, Stanford University Press.

Fisher, Roger & Ury, William(1981) *Getting to Yes: Negotiating Agreement Without Giving In,* London, Hutchinson.

Gilovich, Thomas (1991) *How we Know What Isn't So: The Fallibility of Human Reason in Everyday Life,* New York, The Free Press.

Gottman, John & Silver, Nan (2015) *The Seven Principles for Making Marriage Work: A Practical Guide from the Country's Foremost Relationship Expert,* New York, Harmony Books.

Heath, Chip & Dan (2007) *Made to Stick: Why Some Ideas Survive and Others Die,* New York, Random House.

Henley, N. M. (1973) Status and sex: Some touching observations. *Bulletin of the Psychonomic Society* 2, 91–93.

Herzberg, Fred (1968) "One More Time, How Do You Motivate Employees?" *Harvard Business Review* 65 (5): 109–120.

Johnstone, Keith (1981) *Impro: Improvisation and the Theatre,* London, Eyre Methuen.

Kahneman, Daniel (2011) *Thinking, Fast and Slow,* London, Allen Lane; New York, Farrar, Strauss & Giroux.

Lemov, Doug, Woolway, Erica, & Yezzi, Katie (2012) *Practice Perfect: 42 Rules for Getting Better at Getting Better,* San Francisco, Jossey-Bass.

Leslie, Ian (2014) *Curious: The Desire to Know and Why Your Future Depends on It*, London, Quercus Editions Ltd.

Miller, George (1956). "The magical number seven, plus or minus two: Some limits on our capacity for processing information." *Psychological Review* 63 (2): 81–97.

Oettingen, Gabriele (2014) *Rethinking Positive Thinking: inside the new science of motivation*, NY Penguin Group.

Pinker, Susan (2015) *The Village Effect: Why Face-to-Face Contact Matters,* London, Atlantic Books.

Robbins, Harvey (1995) *Why Teams Don't Work: What went wrong and how to make it right*, Princeton NJ, Petersons/ Pacesetter Books.

Schwartz, Barry (2004) *The Paradox of Choice: Why More is Less,* New York, HarperCollins.

Summerhayes, Diana L. & Suchner Robert W. (1978) Power implications of touch in male—Female relationships, *Sex Roles, Volume 4, Issue 1*, pp 103–110.

Tavris, Carol and Aronson, Elliot (2007) *Mistakes were made (but not by me): Why we justify foolish beliefs, bad decisions and hurtful acts*, New York, Harcourt Brace.

Young, Peter (2003) *Understanding NLP: Principles and Practice*, Carmarthen, Crown House Publishing.

Filmography

Chinatown – Robert Towne (1974)
Days of Wine and Roses – Blake Edwards (1962)
The War of the Roses – Danny DeVito (1999)

Blogs & Web References

The Abilene Paradox – Jerry B Harvey (1988)
- http://www.rmastudies.org.nz/documents/
  AbileneParadoxJerryHarvey.pdf
- http://en.wikipedia.org/wiki/Abilene_paradox

Burkeman, Oliver (2015) Could you be the next Mark Zuckerberg? The Guardian 6 November 2015 http://www.theguardian.com/lifeandstyle/2015/nov/06/zuckerberg-facebook-next-big-idea

Domestic Violence – Clare Murphy (2012)
http://speakoutloud.net/myths-about-domestic-violence/belief-in-a-just-world/cognitive-dissonance-family-violence

Eye-Rolling
Tara Parker-Pope (2002) Can Eye-Rolling Ruin a Marriage? Researchers Study Divorce Risk
http://www.wsj.com/articles/SB1028578553586958760

Fear of Missing Out
https://en.wikipedia.org/wiki/Fear_of_missing_out

Suzannah Hills (2013)
http://www.dailymail.co.uk/news/article-2268092/Whatever-happened-lunch-hour-How-breaks-reduced-just-29-minutes-busy.html

Rana el Kaliouby – TED(2015)
http://www.ted.com/talks/rana_el_kaliouby_this_app_knows_how_you_feel_from_the_look_on_your_face

Mary Matalin and Democrat James Carval – LA Times (2009)

• 	http://latimesblogs.latimes.com/washington/2009/12/mary-matalin-james-carville-marriage.html

Lunch Breaks – OfficeTeam (2014)
http://officeteam.rhi.mediaroom.com/lunchbreaks

Paul Saffo 07.26.2008
http://www.saffo.com/02008/07/26/strong-opinions-weakly-held/